W9-BUJ-239

TUTANKHAMUN

And the Golden Treasures of Ancient Egypt

Publisher and Creative Director: Nick Wells
Project Editor: Christine Kidney
Picture Research: Victoria Lyle and Gemma Walters
Art Director: Mike Spender
Digital Design and Production: Chris Herbert
Layout Design: Dave Jones

First published in 2007 by
STAR FIRE BOOKS
Crabtree Hall, Crabtree Lane
Fulham, London SW6 6TY
United Kingdom

www.star-fire.co.uk

Star Fire is part of The Foundry Creative Media Company Limited

07 09 11 10 08

1 3 5 7 9 10 8 6 4 2

A copy of the CIP data for this book is available from the British Library.

ISBN: 978 1 84451 981 1

PICTURE CREDITS:
Corbis: 1, 4, 5 (t & br), 7 (r), 9, 10, 19 (r), 34 (l), 37 (l), 39 (l), 41, 44 (l & r), 45, 48 (l), 73, 78, 83 (r), 97, 98, 119, 120, 124, 125 (r), 130 (l), 131, 132, 138–139, 170 (l), 171, 178, 180, 181; **Shutterstock**: 5 (bl), 8–9, 15, 22–23, 46–47, 50–51, 52 (l), 80–81, 84–85, 86–87, 88, 104–105, 108, 112–113, 122–123, 134–135, 136, 137, 144–145, 146, 148 (l), 152–153, 156–157, 160–161, 166–167, 169 (r), 172–173, 175, 192, 195, 196, 197; **TopFoto**: 1, 11, 12–13, 14, 19 (l), 79 (r), 102–103, 126 (l), 143 (r & l), 151, 158, 161, 165 (r & l), 170 (b), 182, 186–187, 188, 190, 191 (t), 198; **Werner Forman Archive**: 20, 49, 53, 56 (l), 59, 68–69, 80, 110–111, 116–117, 125 (l), 126–127, 128–129, 130 (r), 133 (b), 134, 141, 142, 154–155, 162–163, 168, 183; Ariadne Gallery, New York: 101; Ashmolean Museum, Oxford: 169 (l), 174, 194 (r), 199; British Museum, London: 7 (l), 60–61, 66–67, 68, 70–71, 93 (r), 114–115, 116, 193; Brooklyn Museum, New York: 24–25; Calouste Gulbenkian Museum, Lisbon: 123, 133 (t), 154; Christie's, London: 150; E. Strouhal: 16–17, 27, 35, 36, 54–55, 62–63, 65, 108–109, 115, 140, 176–177, 189; Egyptian Museum, Cairo: 3, 4 (c & t), 6, 21, 26 (l & r), 28–29, 30, 31, 32–33, 34 (r), 38, 39 (r), 40, 47, 48 (r), 52 (r), 56 (r), 64, 74 (b & t), 76, 77, 79 (l), 82, 83 (l), 85, 90–91, 93 (l), 94 (b & l), 95, 96, 98–99, 106 (l & r), 118, 121, 149, 159, 164, 179, 191 (b), 194 (l), 200; Egyptian Museum, Turin: 42, 57; Fitzwilliam Museum, Cambridge: 89; Louvre, Paris: 75, 92, 147; Luxor Museum, Egypt: 18; Nicholas Reeves, London: 37 (r); Petrie Museum, University College, London: 72; Royal Museum of Art and History, Brussels: 43; Schimmel Collection, New York: 58, 100, 184–185; Schultz Collection, New York: 107

Printed in China

Brenda Ralph Lewis **(author)** fulfilled a childhood ambition to become a writer and has since written well over 100 books and hundreds of articles for British and American magazines. She has also written radio scripts and television documentaries. Brenda specializes in history, and in particular the history of great civilizations. This includes books on Ancient Egypt, Ancient Rome, the Vikings, the Aztecs of Mexico and the Incas of Peru, and a biography of Sir Winston Churchill. Brenda is married and lives in Chesham, Buckinghamshire with her husband. They have one son.

Ian Shaw **(foreword)** is senior lecturer in Egyptian Archaeology at the School of Archaeology, Classics and Egyptology, University of Liverpool. His publications include *Egyptian Warfare and Weapons, The Oxford History of Ancient Egypt* and *Ancient Egypt: A Very Short Introduction*.

TUTANKHAMUN

And the Golden Treasures of Ancient Egypt

BRENDA RALPH LEWIS

with a foreword by IAN SHAW

STAR FIRE

Contents

Foreword

Archaeology is one of the few disciplines that attracts a level of popular interest not commonly associated with academia, and the study of Ancient Egypt in particular has gained a strong grip on the popular imagination. Long before the discovery of the tomb of Tutankhamun, nineteenth-century poets and novelists, such as Percy Shelley and Rider Haggard, were already presenting a romantic view of Ancient Egypt that was very much inspired by the new writings of the adventurers and archaeologists who had begun to publish the first detailed accounts of the pyramids, the Valley of the Kings and the temples of Karnak and Luxor.

The archaeology of pharaonic Egypt, from prehistory to the arrival of Alexander the Great, covers three thousand years (*c.* 3100–332 BC) and museums throughout the world contain millions of Egyptian antiquities. A far greater quantity of objects and monuments are still to be found in Egypt itself, including the temples, cemeteries and cities of the Nile valley and the northern delta region, as well as traces of human life spread across the various deserts from the Sahara to Sinai. The virtually unique survival of this plethora of information about one of the world's first great civilizations has happened for a number of crucial reasons, such as the ancient Egyptians' invention of a unique writing system, their preference for vast and highly decorated funerary monuments and, finally, the fact that their arid climate ensured that some of these writings and monuments were preserved almost intact to the present day.

The major contribution made by Egyptologists to the discipline of archaeology as a whole is the continuous flood of fantastically preserved finds of many kinds. This rapidly expanding database has provided new insights into the material culture of Ancient Egypt, but, perhaps more importantly, it has also made a significant contribution to the creation of a chronological framework for the Mediterranean region. The central role played by Egyptology in the formulation of ancient chronology has lent greater significance to recent attempts to pinpoint flaws in the chronology of the pharaonic period. However, the established chronology is now a very complex mass of archaeological and textual details that has proved very difficult to reassess.

Opinions differ as to the historical moment when simple enthusiasm for Egyptian objects became transformed into the basis of the modern academic discipline of Egyptology. Most would agree, however, that the Napoleonic expedition at the beginning of the nineteenth century was the first systematic attempt to record and describe the standing remains of pharaonic Egypt. The importance of the *Description de l'Égypte* – the multi-volume publication that resulted from the expedition – lay not only in its high standards of draughtsmanship and accuracy but also in the fact that it constituted a continuous and internally consistent appraisal by a single group of scholars, thus providing the first real assessment of ancient Egypt in its totality. Almost all of the subsequent nineteenth-century excavators in Egypt were funded by private collectors and the nascent national museums of Europe and America, all of whom did so in order to obtain Egyptian treasures such as mummies, coffins, sculptures and jewellery. Even in the late nineteenth century, when scholarly societies, such as the Egypt Exploration Fund and the Institut Français d'Archéologie Orientale, began to fund excavations with specific research aims in mind, there were still sponsors requiring a steady stream of antiquities.

However, the real emergence of Egyptology as a fully rounded historical discipline, incorporating the study of both texts and archaeology, was only brought into being by the linguistic endeavours of Jean-François Champollion and Thomas Young. Champollion's decipherment of Egyptian hieroglyphs in 1822, closely followed by Thomas Young's decipherment of the demotic script in the late 1820s, suddenly wrenched Egypt from the twilight of prehistory into a blinding daylight peopled by real historical individuals. It was this understanding of a wide variety of

texts, containing such information as the names of gods and kings as well as the details of religious rituals and economic transactions, that allowed Egyptology finally to become a fully fledged academic pursuit on a par with the more venerable study of the Greek and Roman civilizations.

If Champollion had lit the blue touchpaper, it was Howard Carter – almost exactly a century after Champollion's decipherment of hieroglyphs – who sent popular interest in Egypt soaring into the stratosphere with the discovery of the tomb of Tutankhamun in 1922.

From a purely Egyptological point of view it might be argued that Carter's discovery was something of a mixed blessing. Although his great predecessors, Flinders Petrie and George Reisner, had made sensational discoveries at certain points in their careers, their principal achievement had been to establish Egyptology as a rigorous, scientific discipline concerned with the pursuit of knowledge rather than objets d'art. However, Carter's discovery of Tutankhamun immediately reinforced the popular view of Egypt as a treasure-hunters' paradise in which sheer persistence might eventually be richly rewarded. After the initial days of euphoria, Carter was to spend the rest of his life cataloguing the funerary equipment he had discovered, and Egyptologists have been dogged ever since by a public willing them to find something even more exciting than an intact royal tomb, and they have often found that their sober scientific agenda is at odds with the popular desire for buried treasure.

When a new tomb ('KV63') was discovered in Egypt's Valley of the Kings in 2005, there was, not unexpectedly, a great deal of coverage of the event in newspapers and on television news bulletins. Inevitably this find was compared with the excavation of the tomb of Tutankhamun, but, equally inevitably perhaps, it rapidly turned out to be a much smaller and far less fabulous find – the coffins contained no actual bodies, and the quantities of funerary goods were not remotely on the scale of those unearthed by Carter over 80 years earlier. By any measure, the tomb of Tutankhamun is a tremendously hard act to follow, and there is a sense in which the popular history of Egyptology from 1922 onwards has been one long succession of anti-climaxes. In another sense, however, it is Tutankhamun's tomb that has in one way or another lured many scholars into the pursuit of Egyptology, and it is the sheer possibility that something like it is still lurking under the sand that brings millions of tourists to the Valley of the Kings, or keeps them glued to their National Geographic and Discovery channels. It is not just Tutankhamun but the possibility of 'another Tutankhamun' that keeps such a wide public engaged with Egyptian archaeology. Above all, the tomb of Tutankhamun is the yard-stick against which all subsequent major discoveries have been measured, and so far they have all fallen short. This book shows why.

Ian Shaw, 2007

Tutankhamun

This is the story of Tutankhamun, who shot to worldwide fame after 1922, when his tomb, more than 3,000 years old, was discovered in the Valley of the Kings in Egypt. Howard Carter, the quiet, scholarly English archaeologist who found the tomb after searching for it for 15 years also became a celebrity. The world was provided with a first-class sensation, complete with stunning treasures and a curse that supposedly killed off members of Carter's expedition as punishment for defiling a pharaoh's tomb. The story of Tutankhamun – and the curse – is still running today, with regular travelling exhibitions of Tutankhamun's treasures, several horror movies dramatizing the Pharaoh's curse in different forms and even sets of postage stamps celebrating the Pharaoh, who has the added emotional appeal of suffering a premature death, aged only 18. If Howard Carter, his sponsor the fifth Earl of Carnarvon and their team transformed Tutankhamun from an obscure ruler of a long-ago land, one known only to archaeologists and amateur enthusiasts, into a world-famous enigmatic icon, they also brought into greater focus the world of the pharaohs with its dazzling wealth, art, architecture, beautiful jewellery and decoration – and its status as the mighty superpower of its time.

The Discovery and Excavation of Tutankhamun's Tomb

THE MOMENT OF TRUTH
Howard Carter's discovery

On 26 November 1922, English archaeologist Howard Carter (1874–1939) stood before a sealed door in the tomb of the Ancient Egyptian Pharaoh Tutankhamun, some nine metres below the rock and sand surface of the Valley of the Kings. It was a thrilling moment, signifying the end of a 15-year search. Carefully Carter made a small hole in the upper left-hand corner of the door, then used a lighted candle to test behind it for noxious gases. There were none. Widening the hole, Carter peered in.

'Can you see anything?' asked Lord Carnarvon, Carter's sponsor, who was standing behind him.

'Yes!' was Carter's reply, 'Wonderful things!'

WHAT HOWARD CARTER SAW
The first glimpse of the treasure

Just how 'wonderful' was revealed when Carter widened the hole still further and inserted an electric torch. Its beam lit up around 700 pieces of the most sumptuous treasure Carter had ever seen. Later, he wrote:

'Three gilt couches ... two life-sized figures [of Tutankhamun] carved in black, the protective sacred cobra upon their foreheads ... between them, around them, piled on top of them ... exquisitely painted and inlaid caskets, alabaster vases ... strange black shrines ... from the open door of one, a great gilt snake peeping out ... a beautiful lotiform cup of translucent calcite ... [four] chariots glistening with gold inlay ...'

TUTANKHAMUN, WORLDWIDE CELEBRITY

The international sensation of the discovery

Four days later, on 30 November, the news broke worldwide of Carter's thrilling find. It was an immediate sensation. Reporters, cameramen, newsreel makers, anyone and everyone who could afford the trip to Egypt were soon converging on the excavations and swarming over every vantage point around them. Carter was infuriated. He was a meticulous, scholarly man who needed privacy and quiet to do his work, but privacy and quiet were the last things he got.

CARTER UNDER SIEGE
The painstaking path to the sarcophagus

This was not the only siege Carter had to undergo. He began to receive up to 20 begging letters per day, requesting souvenirs and other favours. All this complicated the next stage – covering artefacts with preservative, photographing, noting, labelling and packing every item from the tomb ready for transport to the Cairo Museum. It was a long and arduous task, but at last, in October 1925, Carter was ready to embark on the greatest adventure of all – opening the sarcophagus that contained the mummified body of the youthful Tutankhamun.

TUTANKHAMUN REVEALED
Unveiling the face of the young Pharaoh

The Pharaoh's mummy lay in the last of three coffins, each slotted neatly into the next. The first was opened on 10 October 1925, the second, which had garlands and a linen shroud on its lid, on 23 October, and the last, three days later. As the lid was lifted, a magnificent golden death mask came into view. It was decorated with inlays of lapis lazuli, carnelian, quartz, obsidian, turquoise and glass. Beneath the mask lay the face of Tutankhamun, wizened, but still recognizable as a face after more than 3,000 years. After the unwrapping of the mummy began on 11 November over 100 objects were found inside. Most were made of gold and included good luck amulets, bracelets, necklaces and two daggers.

THE CURSE OF TUTANKHAMUN

Twentieth-century legend

The Tutankhamun sensation was greatly increased by the rumours, stoked up by the press, that there was a curse on his tomb. The first 'victim' was Lord Carnarvon, who died on 5 April 1923 after an insect bite turned septic and pneumonia developed. By 1939, another twenty members of the expedition were mysteriously or violently dead. But Howard Carter, the most likely candidate for death, escaped and poured scorn on the very idea of a curse.

Carter continued to work on his great find and in February 1932, after nearly ten years, sent the last of the 3,500 artefacts found in the tomb to the Cairo Museum, where they remain to this day.

Tutankhamun at Amarna

TUTANKHATEN
The origins of Tutankhamun

When the tomb of Tutankhamun was discovered in 1922, he was one of the least known of the pharaohs of Ancient Egypt. Subsequent research into his brief life revealed that he was probably born at Tel-el-Amarna some 280 km (174 m) south of Cairo in around 1345 BC. At first the future pharaoh was known as Tutankhaten, 'living image of the Sun god Aten', who had been championed as the sole deity of Egypt by Amenhotep IV (1352–1336 BC). For this, Amenhotep (shown left), who changed his own name to Akhenaten, was condemned as a heretic.

LIKE FATHER, LIKE SON
A shared genetic history

Akhenaten was certainly Tutankhamun's father-in-law but may also have been his father. A blood relationship was likely since both appeared to display physical symptoms of the genetic disorder Marfan's Syndrome. In Marfan's, the connective tissue supporting tendons, blood vessel walls or heart valves is weakened. Sufferers are often tall and thin, with tapering fingers, long arms and legs, curvature of the spine and elongated heads. Tutankhamun's mummy revealed that he had several of these physical traits – he had long legs and was unusually tall, as was Akhenaten.

NATURE AND ART
Akhenaten's break with tradition

Religion was not the only aspect of Ancient Egyptian life that was changed by Akhenaten. Previously, Egyptian art had been highly stylized, with traditional, usually flattering ways of depicting the royal family. Flowers, trees and other aspects of Nature were presented in artificial ways. The god Aten was frequently featured in relief (though not in sculpture). Akhenaten allowed his thin, elongated face – another sign of Marfan's syndrome – to be shown in his portraits. Flowers, trees, plants, animals and their settings were depicted in natural rather than artificial forms. For example, on the wall of a building called Maru-Aten at Tell-el-Amarna a flock of ducks flying out of a papyrus thicket was painted much as they might have been seen in the Nile delta in ancient times.

HUSBAND AND WIFE
A poignant depiction of family life

Tutankhamun married at a very young age. If, as some archaeologists believe, his father was Akhenaten, then his wife, Ankhesenamun, one of Akhenaten's six daughters by his queen, Nefertiti, would have been his half-sister. Tutankhamun's mother is thought to have been Queen Tiy, one of Akhenaten's minor wives. Paintings found in Tutankhamun's tomb reveal that he and his wife had a very affectionate relationship. She is seen offering him flowers and there are smiles on their faces. Sadly, both of their two children were miscarried. Their foetuses were discovered in their father's tomb.

THE TEMPLE OF KARNAK

Akhenaten's devotion to Aten

Tell-el-Amarna replaced Luxor as the capital city of Ancient Egypt during the reign of Akhenaten (1352–1336 BC). It was given over almost entirely to the worship of the god Aten. Tell-el-Amarna was founded in about 1350 BC. Soon after, Akhenaten built a temple to Aten at Karnak. This was followed in Tell-el-Amarna by several more temples, palaces and extensive areas of mud brick housing. The whole site, laid out on a plain by the east bank of the River Nile, measured some 10 km (6¼ m) long by 5 km (3 m) wide.

AKHENATEN

Return to Luxor

Tell-el-Amarna was not occupied for long. It was abandoned after the death of Akhenaten, when Amun and Luxor were restored to their former positions. The worship of Aten was outlawed and the very name of Akhenaten, the heretic, was defaced from his statues, and even from the seals on his tomb.

Tutankhamun as Pharaoh

CHANGING THE ROYAL NAME
Tutankhaten becomes Tutankhamun

Tutankhamun was a boy when he succeeded to the throne of Ancient Egypt. After the death of Akhenaten there was a brief rule of about three years by Semenkhkare, whose identity remains something of a mystery. When the young boy eventually became Pharaoh, almost at once he decided, or was told to, abandon the worship of Aten and reinstate Amun as state god. This required a change of the royal name. Tutankhaten duly became Tutankhamun and his wife Ankhesenpaaten became Ankhesenamun. The 'natural' Amarna style of art was also changed so that royal portraits reverted to more flattering portraits in which every face, male and female, took on the standard 'pretty', slightly feminine aspect.

THE ROYAL CROOK AND FLAIL
Symbols of Ancient Egyptian royalty

During their coronation, Ancient Egyptian pharaohs carried the crook and flail as symbols of their power and responsibility. The priests performing the coronation ceremony for the young Tutankhamun would have placed child-sized crowns and head coverings on his head – one the low red crown of Lower Egypt, another the high white crown of Upper Egypt and afterwards the blue crown, the striped nemes headcloth and plain head covering.

THE WARRIOR BOY KING
The weapons of war

Tutankhamun came from a long line of warrior pharaohs, many of whom had personally led their troops into battle against the enemies of Egypt. However extreme, youth was not a consideration when ensuring that a pharaoh was trained to be a warrior and presented a military face not only to his enemies, but to his subjects. Of the six chariots found in Tutankhamun's tomb, five were probably for use in battle. There were also almost fifty bows, arrows, slingshots and other weapons.

HIGH PRIEST
Tutankhamun as god

Tutankhamun was much more than the ruler of Ancient Egypt. Another of his functions was to act as high priest of the gods. In this role, he rebuilt and endowed the temples of the gods and made offerings to them. All of it was funded at Tutankhamun's expense. Tutankhamun also made his own images of the gods, from electrum and semiprecious stones. Several monuments from the reign of Tutankhamun were discovered at Karnak and at Nubia. Thebes, the traditional capital of Upper and Lower Egypt, proved to be the source of most stone statues featuring Tutankhamun's face, many of them in the guise of various gods.

SINS OF THE FATHER
The restoration of Amun

There was a particularly good reason why Tutankhamun was so involved with the gods of Ancient Egypt. The heresy of Akhenaten, which had displaced the god Amun from his place as official state god had to be publicly expunged and Amun had to be formally recognized once again. This was done at a special ceremony at the Temple of Karnak which the boy pharaoh attended stripped to the waist, his feet bare and his only garment a simple loincloth. He was met by priests wearing masks the gods representing and had to undergo purification ceremonies which formally restored the link between the pharaoh and the god Amun.

THE SPORTS OF KINGS

Hunting ostrich

Sport has always been a favourite relaxation of kings and pharaohs and Tutankhamun was no exception. Among the magnificent finds made at his tomb after 1922, there was a 'fan' made of gold which featured him sitting in a chariot, taking part in an ostrich hunt. Duck hunting was another of the young Pharaoh's activities. On one of the panels in the Golden Shrine found in his tomb, Tutankhamun was shown with his kill, a wild duck, hanging down dead with the Pharaoh's arrow through it.

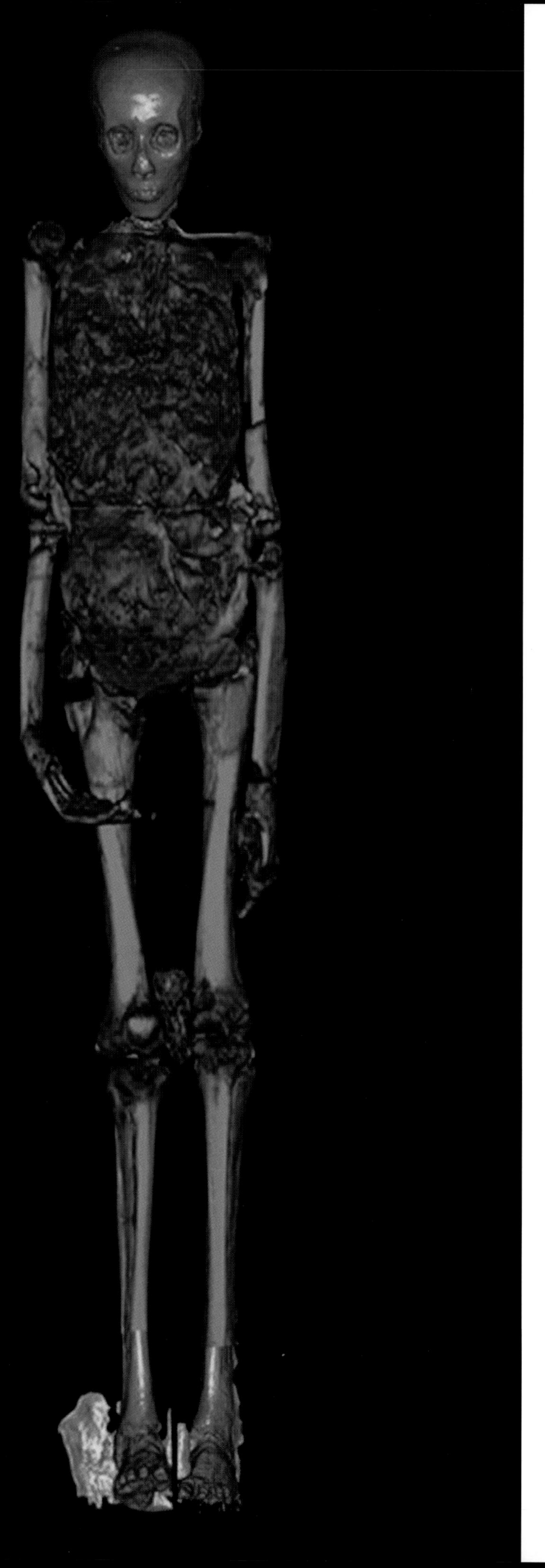

The Death and Burial of Tutankhamun

THE DEATH OF TUTANKHAMUN
Edging towards the cause

Tutankhamun died tragically young, when he was only around 18 years old. After his tomb was discovered in 1922, there were rumours that the youthful pharaoh had been murdered. One suggested culprit was his powerful adviser Ay, who afterwards succeeded him on the throne of Egypt (1327–1323 BC). The evidence, it seems, lay in damage to Tutankhamun's skull, which was said to have been the result of a heavy blow. However, in 2005, a team of Egyptologists concluded from new evidence, provided by new X-rays and scans, that foul play was not involved. Instead Tutankhamun died from a broken leg which turned gangrenous.

PASSAGE INTO THE AFTERLIFE
Preserving the body of the Pharaoh

The Ancient Egyptians have often been accused of an obsessive interest in death. Rather, they were obsessed with life and how to continue it in the next world. For this purpose, a vital prerequisite was the preservation of the body. Only by this means could the deceased arrive in the afterlife in the proper condition to resume and enjoy his earthly existence. The process that preserved the deceased was mummification.

HOW TO MUMMIFY A PHARAOH

Stage one

Mummification began with drawing out the pharaoh's brain through his nostrils, using a metal hook. Next, drugs rinsed out the brain cavity and removed any residual matter. Then an incision was made in the pharaoh's side and through this, his internal organs were removed. The cavity was then washed out with a mixture of palm oil and powdered spices and the incision was sewn up. Organs were set aside for separate burial within the pharaoh's tomb.

HOW TO MUMMIFY A PHARAOH

Stage two

The next step was to marinate the body in the mineral salt natron. It took seventy days for the natron to mummify the body. After that, the corpse was washed and wrapped from head to toe in fine linen bandages rubbed with gum. After this, the body was given to the family of the deceased to be placed in a human-shaped coffin which was propped against a wall inside the burial chamber.

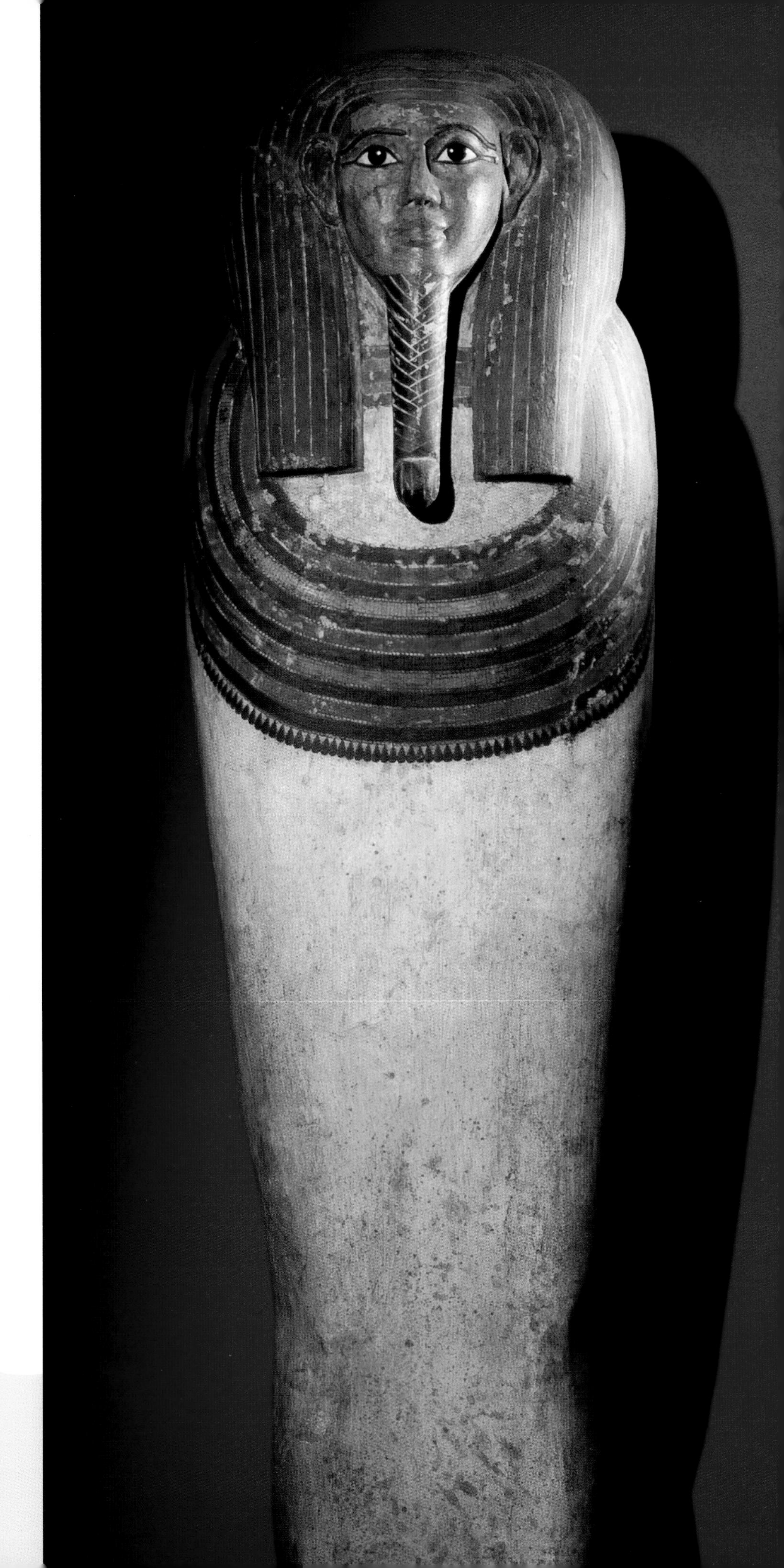

ALL THEIR WORLDLY GOODS
Why the tombs yielded such treasures

Since the Ancient Egyptians conceived the afterlife as a reflection of life on Earth, they packed the tomb of the pharaohs or other eminent personages with all their possessions for use in their next life. This belief accounts for the splendid treasures which the tombs of the pharaohs contained and which were such a great temptation to tomb robbers, both ancient and modern, and why the discoveries made there came in every possible variety. Furniture, carriages, weapons, clothes, jewellery as well as personal possessions such as games and cosmetics were all included in a pharaoh's funerary equipment. A quantity of readymade food was also provided, but when this ran out, pictures of various dishes, fruits or vegetables, painted on the walls of the tomb, were supposed to come to life and renew the supply.

SERVANTS IN DEATH
Domestic service in the afterlife

Provision was made for pharaohs and other high-ranking Egyptians to enjoy the services of servants for tasks that were too lowly and menial for them to perform. Figurines called *shabtis* were buried in the tombs. This custom started in the Middle Kingdom and is closely linked to the Osiris cult. Every deceased person who managed to enter the fields of reed (the realm of Osiris and comparable to our paradise) was expected to perform agricultural tasks. These tasks (taken over by the *shabtis*) were performed for Osiris. The *shabtis* took the place of the deceased.

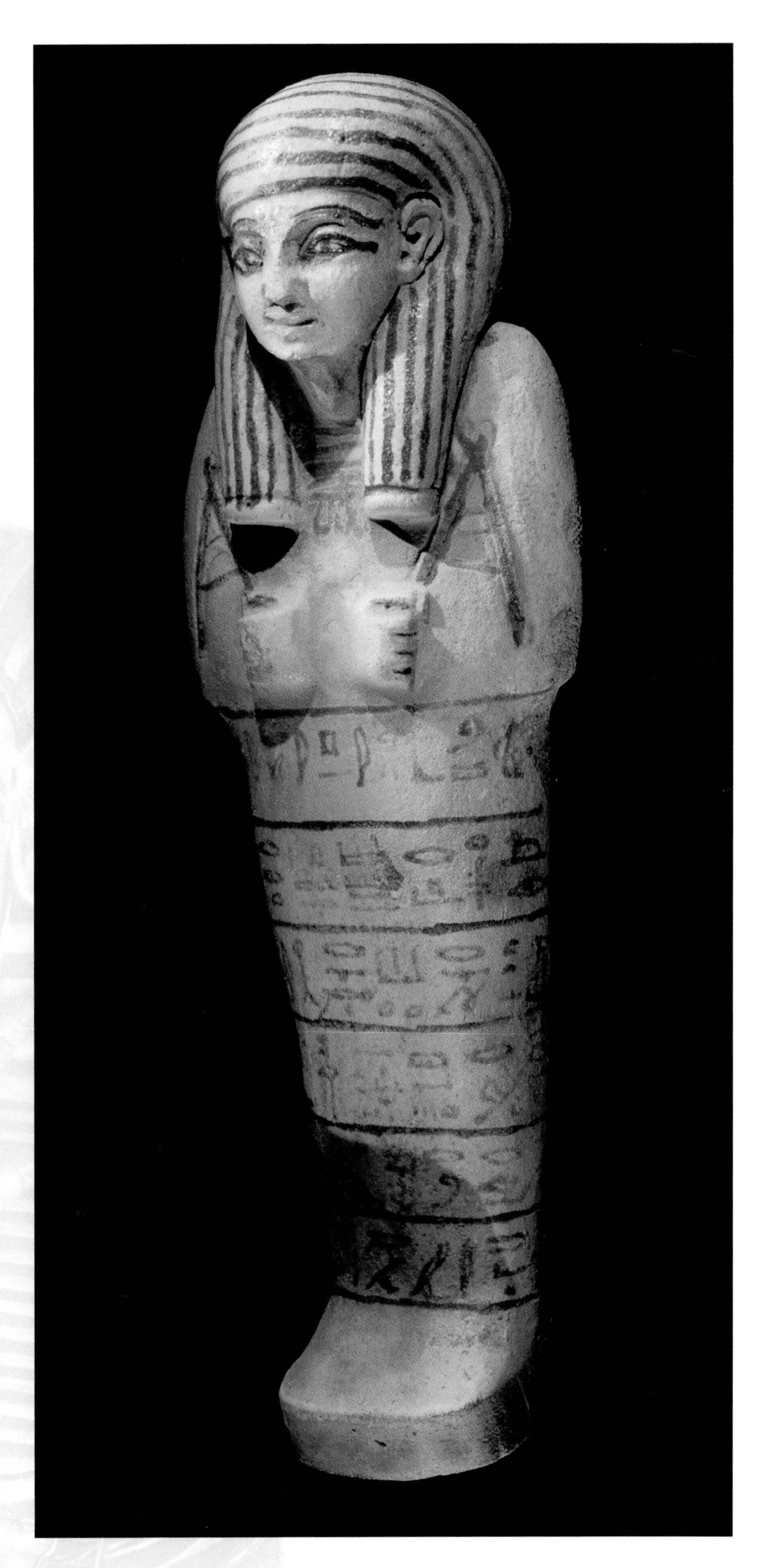

The Treasures of Tutankhamun

GOOD LUCK CHARMS
The scarab beetle

This pectoral (left) with a winged scarab at its centre and the sun disk above was designed to be worn on the chest by both men and women. Pectorals were a common piece of jewellery in Ancient Egypt. Their size allowed for plenty of colourful decoration and for the addition of numerous good luck charms, which were regarded as essential in this very superstitious society. The scarab beetle, one of many types of amulet, was particularly valued and frequently worn as a symbol of rebirth.

THE JACKAL-FORM GOD
Anubis the protector

This statue of Anubis (right), in full jackal form, was found in Tutankhamun's tomb. In Ancient Egypt dogs and jackals were often found around the edges of the desert, especially near the cemeteries where the dead were buried. In fact, the Egyptians may even have begun the practice of making elaborate graves and tombs to protect the dead from desecration by jackals. Anubis was the guardian of the dead, who greeted the souls in the Underworld and protected them on their journey, so it is not surprising that Tutankhamun had his own Anubis to protect him on his way to the afterlife. Often Anubis is presented as a jackal-headed man rather than a fully dog-shaped creature.

ANCIENT EGYPTIAN SKIN CARE
The contents of a cosmetic jar

The Ancient Egyptians, both male and female, treated their skin with creams and oils, which were kept in jars like these ones. It was a sensible precaution in a hot, dry land like Egypt, where the boiling Sun, shining out of a clear, open sky, day after day, could wreak dangerous damage. Many such decorative jars found by archaeologists still contained traces of their original contents – animal fats and vegetable resins.

ANCIENT EGYPTIAN EYELINER
The protective qualities of kohl

The most distinguishing feature of Ancient Egyptian cosmetics, seen in paintings and other images of both sexes, was eye make-up in which the eye was surrounded by black kohl. Kohl was called *mesdemet* in Ancient Egypt and was based on the grey or black mineral known as galena or lead sulphide. It was mixed into a paste with water and applied with the fingers or a kohl 'pencil'. Kohl also had a protective purpose: Ancient Egyptians believed that it protected the eyes from the glare of the sun.

GOLDEN ARTISTRY
The canopic coffinette of Tutankhamun

The small 'coffinettes' and 'canopic jars' found in Ancient Egyptian tombs, including Tutankhamun's, were used to hold the embalmed internal organs of the deceased. The Egyptians believed that in the afterlife the separated parts of the body would magically come together and the dead person would join together and be whole again. The coffinettes found in the tomb of Tutankhamun were made of solid gold and have been classed as great examples of Egyptian artistry.

FURNISHING THE AFTERLIFE
Tutankhamun's chairs

This beautiful folding stool, with a seat made of ebony inlaid with ivory, was one among the numerous items of furniture found in the tomb of Tutankhamun. Other seating, in the form of thrones and chairs, was also included. The Ancient Egyptians believed that in the next world, the pharaoh could furnish his new home with the furniture he had brought with him and re-start his life as though he had never died.

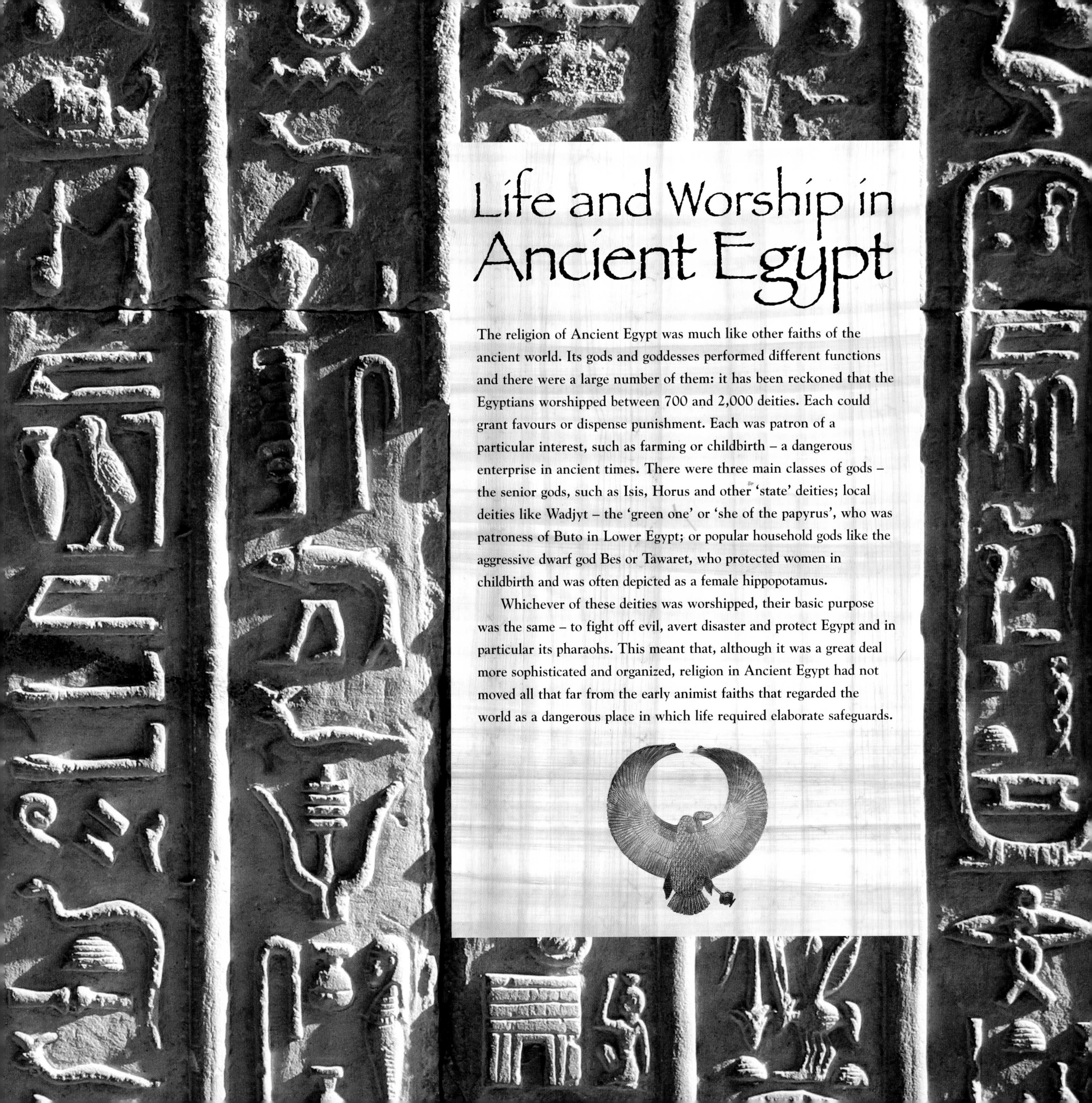

Life and Worship in Ancient Egypt

The religion of Ancient Egypt was much like other faiths of the ancient world. Its gods and goddesses performed different functions and there were a large number of them: it has been reckoned that the Egyptians worshipped between 700 and 2,000 deities. Each could grant favours or dispense punishment. Each was patron of a particular interest, such as farming or childbirth – a dangerous enterprise in ancient times. There were three main classes of gods – the senior gods, such as Isis, Horus and other 'state' deities; local deities like Wadjyt – the 'green one' or 'she of the papyrus', who was patroness of Buto in Lower Egypt; or popular household gods like the aggressive dwarf god Bes or Tawaret, who protected women in childbirth and was often depicted as a female hippopotamus.

Whichever of these deities was worshipped, their basic purpose was the same – to fight off evil, avert disaster and protect Egypt and in particular its pharaohs. This meant that, although it was a great deal more sophisticated and organized, religion in Ancient Egypt had not moved all that far from the early animist faiths that regarded the world as a dangerous place in which life required elaborate safeguards.

The Religion of Ancient Egypt

PHARAOH AS GOD
Preserving order

The pharaohs of Ancient Egypt were a great deal more than rulers. They were also partners with the gods in the practice of the Egyptian religion. Pharaohs were frequently represented as gods. For instance, the picture on the left illustrates Tutankhamun as Nefertem, god of the lotus flower, which was the symbol of Upper Egypt. The religion of Ancient Egypt were primarily concerned with fending off chaos that could destroy the divine order. Maintaining that order was paramount and was achieved by strict adherence to the rules of *maat*, which comprised truth, justice and the harmony of the universe.

SACRED LAKES
Cleanliness and godliness

As in many religions, both ancient and modern, worshippers were duty bound to keep themselves ritually clean. In Ancient Egypt, one of the ways this was achieved was by immersion in a sacred lake. Sacred lakes were artificial stretches of pure water constructed within the environs of Ancient Egyptian temples. One such lake, rectangular in shape and lined with stone, was built at the Temple of Amun at Karnak. Among their other religious purposes, sacred lakes provided homes for sacred geese or crocodiles.

THE BATTLING GOD

Tutankhamun as Horus

Another of Tutankhamun's religious disguises was as the god Horus. In an 'action' statue found in his tomb, he was shown about to attack evil with a long harpoon. Horus was usually depicted wearing the head of a falcon or as a falcon himself. The son of the deities Isis and Osiris, Horus was among the earliest of Egyptian gods, worshipped from around 3100 BC when the very First Dynasty came to power.

THE KING OF HELIOPOLIS
The cartouche

In Ancient Egypt, the elliptical cartouche symbolized the circuit of the sun. A chest in the shape of a cartouche found in Tutankhamun's tomb featured his name, inlaid on the top in ebony and ivory, as the 'King of Heliopolis' (King of the City of the Sun). The cartouche had important spiritual meaning, signifying all-round protection. The elliptical shape was essentially a longer version of the circular hieroglyphic *shen*, which denoted infinity. Where *shen* was depicted encircling the sun, it seems to have been indicating the eternity of the universe.

OSIRIS
Goddess of Devotion

The story of the Egyptian goddess Isis and her brother-husband Osiris was the most poignant tale of love and devotion among the mythologies of the ancient world. After Osiris, god of death, resurrection and fertility, was killed and dismembered by Seth, god of confusion and chaos, Isis searched the world for his body-parts and put them back together again. In the process, Isis breathed life back into Osiris and also conceived their son Horus. Osiris and Seth were brothers and Isis was their sister. The marital status of Isis and Osiris probably influenced the practice of marriage between brothers and sisters in the royal family.

ETERNAL LIFE

Ritual in Ancient Egypt

The religious beliefs of ordinary Egyptians centred around two important factors. The first was that death did not mean the end of life, only a temporary interruption. The other was that life could be made eternal by certain ritual acts. Mummification of the body was one of these acts, another was an attitude of piety towards the gods. There was also the belief that individuals comprised three important elements, apart from the physical body. These were Ka, Ba and Ankh – the creative life force, the personality and life itself.

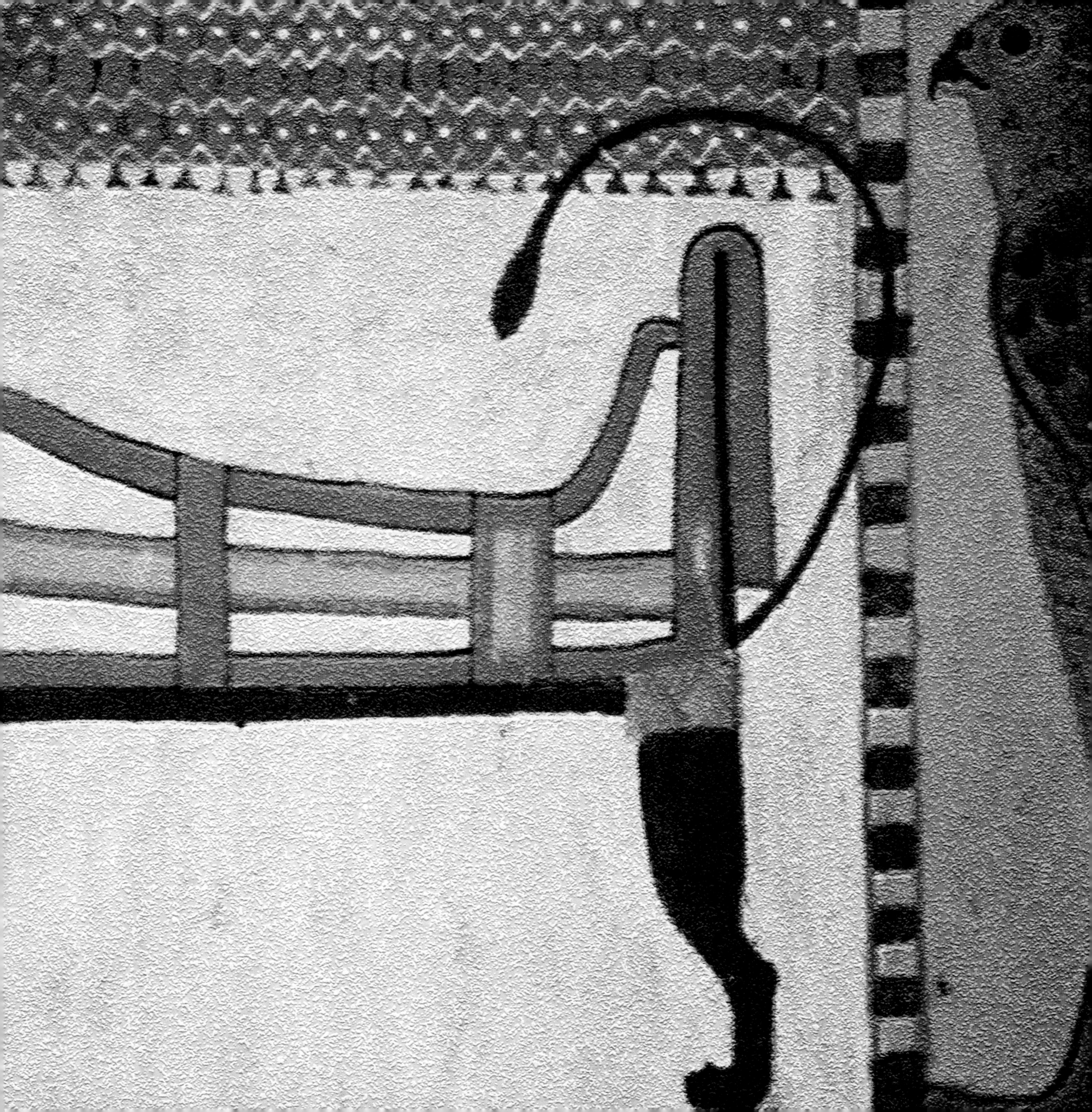

Food for the Pharaoh

THE ANCIENT EGYPTIAN DIET
Depiction of food

The pictures of various foods painted on the walls of tombs in the Valley of the Kings and elsewhere, together with lifelike sculptures of fruits, vegetables, bread or fowl revealed a great deal of information about the Ancient Egyptian diet. The land on either side of the River Nile – an extended oasis in the middle of arid desert – made Egypt an extremely fertile land with a wealth of fruits, vegetables, meats and fish available to eat.

LUXURY FOODS
The rich–poor divide

The pharaohs, the high officials, aristocrats and other high-ranking personages, together with their families, naturally had access to the finest foods. As depicted in Ancient Egyptian tombs, these would have included various types of meat and fowl that were luxuries for most ordinary people. Most meat came from the temples, where cattle served as sacrifices to the gods, although farmers also raised pigs for food. What was a luxury for the upper classes was a rare treat for the mass of Egyptians, who usually tasted meat only at important religious festivals. Ordinary Egyptians were mostly only able to eat meat in the form of hares, gazelles and other wild animals. Symbolic of the social divide between rich and poor in Ancient Egypt, these same animals were hunted by the wealthy for sport.

THE EGYPTIAN DIET

What most Egyptians ate

The basic diet of ordinary Egyptians consisted of bread and beer. The beer was not necessarily a strongly alcoholic drink, but was more like a thick, nutritious soup. Sometimes, the beer was made sweeter by the addition of dates and other fruits. The Egyptian diet was augmented by various pulses and vegetables such as garlic, lentils, onions, beans, cucumber and lettuce. Salted fish, which was cheaper than meat, was another important item on the table. Grapes were used to make wine, and a wide range of fruits was available for most people – figs, dates, pomegranates, palm nut and occasionally almonds, which were rare.

TUTANKHAMUN'S PACKED LUNCH

Howard Carter's discovery of food

The Ancient Egyptians were, it seems, familiar with packed lunches. In the antechamber of Tutankhamun's tomb, Howard Carter and his team discovered a pile of boxes. These contained ready-cooked and prepared meats in egg-shaped boxes. Black resin had been poured inside the boxes, presumably to preserve the meat. The boxes were discovered stacked underneath a couch, which depicted a cow.

ANIMALS AS LUXURY

Food as currency

Animals, of course, performed numerous functions on the farms of Ancient Egypt. Among them was their contribution to the food supply, not only as meat, but also as a source of fat and oils for cooking. Cows provided milk. Eggs were provided by ducks. These items were also treated as 'currency'.

DAILY BREAD
Egypt's plentiful crops

As in most countries, bread was central to the staple diet of Ancient Egyptians. Most bread was generally made from emmer wheat but other grains such as barley and spelt wheat, were also used. These grains were unlikely to be in short supply for the rich soil of Egypt and the plentiful supply of water for irrigation meant that it was possible to produce crops twice a year. Texts written on ostraca (shards of pottery or flakes of limestone), which were found at the village of Deir-el-Medina, a settlement on the west bank of the Nile opposite Thebes, indicated that workmen's pay took the form of grain.

Entertaining the Pharaoh

BOARD GAMES

Tutankhamun's game of senet

The Ancient Egyptians were very fond of games, some of them allied to death and burial rituals. *Senet*, or the 'game of passing', may have represented a journey through the afterlife. Tutankhamun was buried with four ivory and ebony *senet* boards. This was probably the most popular game and was played either on inlaid boards, like chess or draughts, or on grids of thirty squares carved or scratched on large stones. There were two players usually with seven playing pieces each. To reach the finishing line and win, apparently involved a series of special squares, which represented good or bad luck. Another game, probably imported from western Asia was 'Twenty Squares', which may have been a cut-down version of *senet*, with two players using five pieces on a 20-square board or grid.

DOGS AND JACKALS

Playing games in the afterlife

'Dogs and Jackals' was another popular board game and several examples have been found in Ancient Egyptian tombs. Played on an ivory board measuring 15 x 10 cm (6 x 4 in), it looked more like a piece of furniture with legs carved into the shapes of animals. A palm tree was also carved into it, together with 55 holes. The pawns, made of ebony, were stored in special drawers. Three dice were used to dictate how the pieces moved and whoever had all the pieces in his or her possession at the end of the game was the winner.

MAKING MUSIC

Ancient Egyptian musical instruments and dance

Music had an important role to play in Ancient Egyptian culture. Tomb paintings showed groups of musicians, either entertaining the guests at banquets on their own or providing an accompaniment for troupes of dancers. There was a wide variety of musical instruments available – ivory clappers, harps, lutes, sistra, cymbals and bells, tambourines, flutes, double clarinets, double oboes and lyres. Egyptian musicians frequently sang to their own accompaniments. Dancers sometimes used castanets to help them maintain the rhythm for their performances. Much of their dancing was athletic, featuring cartwheels or handstands.

COOLING HATS
Nard in a hot climate

Ancient Egypt had a broilingly hot climate, with very little, if any, regular rainfall. In fact, but for the Nile, the country would never have been able to exist. Methods of cooling down were therefore vital and one of these was a cone of nard, made from aromatic oils. Guests at banquets placed these cones on their heads and during the meal, the nard melted all over their heads, faces and shoulders, producing a pleasant cooling effect.

EGYPTIAN BALL GAMES
Outdoor games

Ancient Egyptians also enjoyed active games that built up their fitness and physique. One of their games was something that resembled an English game called 'tipcat', in which the ball had to be kept in the air. They used long palm tree branches for sticks and the ball was made from two pieces of leather stuffed with papyrus leaves. Rubber was unknown in Ancient Egypt, so ball games had to be played with leather filled with chaff, dry papyrus reeds, string or rags, all tied tightly together.

HUNTING
Action in the afterlife

Wall paintings and other depictions buried in Ancient Egyptian tombs presumed that every activity which the deceased had enjoyed continued regardless after death and burial. Although a break in contact was acknowledged by filling the tombs of dead Egyptians with all their wordly possessions ready for when they were able to use them again, the break did not, apparently, include family activities. There was, for example, a wall painting from around 1400 BC, found in a tomb at Thebes, showing a dead man in the Nile marshes sharing a bird hunt with his family.

Clothing and Jewellery in Ancient Egypt

DRESSING FOR THE HOT WEATHER

Clothes light and simple

As might be expected in a country as hot as Ancient Egypt, the clothes worn by both men and women were simple and light. The earliest surviving Egyptian garment, dated at 2980 BC, is a long-sleeved V-necked shirt with a pleated yoke, made of linen and measuring 58 cm (23 in) in length that was found in 1912 at Tarkhan in Lower Egypt. Generally, the clothes worn by farmers were much more skimpy than this – just a loincloth and little else. Although the loincloth was a very basic fashion, mainly confined to poorer Egyptians, it appears that Tutankhamun wore it as well: three triangular linen loincloths were found in his tomb.

WOMEN'S SHEATH DRESSES

Simple but colourful

Women generally wore a simple sheath dress, with one or two broad shoulder straps. However, the fabrics of which they were made were often brightly coloured, beautifully patterned and worn by wealthier women with a covering of bead netting. By the reign of Amenhotep III (1390–1352 BC), the father of Akhenaten, tunics had become decidedly daring: fashioned from thin, diaphonous fabrics, they were virtually transparent.

TUTANKHAMUN'S WARDROBE
Dressing for the afterlife

A substantial wardrobe was found in the Tomb of Tutankhamun. The materials used were sumptuous – linen decorated with gold thread or colourful beading. But pharaohs were not the only Egyptians to be buried with all their clothes to wear in the afterlife. Kha, the chief architect of Thebes during the 18th, was buried with 26 knee-length shirts and some 50 loincloths, some of them made of leather. Kha's wardrobe for the winter included 17 heavy linen tunics.

FASHION IN ANCIENT EGYPT
Dressed to advertise status

Some of the government officials whose tombs have been found in Egypt were buried with clothes or statues and other images that indicated their status in life. The statue of a vizier or chief adviser, for example, wore a long robe. A priest was usually depicted wearing a leopard skin. The upper echelons of Ancient Egyptian society – courtiers and such – were fashion-conscious and like all fashion, this could change from season to season. This occurred so regularly that archaeologists found it possible to use fashions as found in tombs to date the period in which they were worn. For example, the discovery of pleated loincloths with fronts arranged like aprons dated the tomb in or around the reign of Rameses II (1279–1213 BC).

JEWELLERY AND ADORNMENT

Showing off in Ancient Egypt

Jewellery, and plenty of it, was a must for a wealthy, socially ambitious society like Ancient Egypt, where the elite was eager to display its eminence. This was why so many early discoveries in the tombs of Ancient Egypt comprised jewellery of one sort or another. Rings, armlets, necklaces, collarettes, bracelets and much more were fashioned in a wide range of precious stones and metals – gold, silver, lapis lazuli, feldspar, cornelian and many more.

JEWELLERY FROM OUTER SPACE

Delivered by meteorite

In the spring of 2006, an unusual piece of news about an artefact from Tutankhamun's tomb hit newspaper headlines. During the original excavations at the tomb in 1922, a necklace was found in which the jewelled decorations included a scarab beetle carved from yellow green glass. The origin of the glass remained a puzzle for the next 85 years until archaeologists put forward a new theory. They believed the glass came from outer space in the form of a meteorite – or, rather, it was created *by* the meteorite. This struck the earth with such superheated force that it melted the sand and sandstone. As the sand cooled, the glass formed.

Protecting the Pharaoh

EVIL EVERYWHERE
Fending off fate

The Ancient Egyptians were virtually obsessed with protection. Evil, they feared, was everywhere. Harm hovered over everyone and everything. Accidents were always waiting to happen. As a result, various Egyptian gods and goddesses were used to provide protection. This was why Howard Carter discovered so many images of deities and goddesses in the tomb of Tutankhamun, together with protective amulets and other lucky signs and symbols. Among them were four goddesses gilded and scantily dressed, guarding the shrine of Tutankhamun: the scorpion goddess Serket; Isis, symbolic mother of the pharaohs; Neith, a creator-goddess and Nephthys, protector of the dead.

TUTANKHAMUN'S PROTECTORS
Statues on guard duty

There could be no doubt as to the purpose of the two statues discovered standing over the entrance to Tutankhamun's burial chamber. Their size, their pose and the weapons they held out in front of the doors had 'Protect the Pharaoh' written all over them. Both statues were made of wood covered in black bitumen, except for their headdresses, front skirts, armlets and sandals, which were covered in gold leaf.

THE SIGN OF THE SEAL

Intact and untouched

A knotted rope with intact seals was the one sign that archaeologists excavating tombs in Egypt most hoped to find. It would have indicated that a tomb had not been entered and pillaged since it was sealed up after a burial. In 1922, Howard Carter was a very lucky man, for in discovering Tutankhamun's tomb, he had found what was then by far the most intact burial place in the Valley. The tomb remained so until 2006, when three Fifth-Dynasty tombs (2494–2345 BC) were discovered at Saqqara, near Cairo.

GODDESSES ON GUARD

The vengeance of Meretseger

Pharaohs of Ancient Egypt had a protector in the goddess Meretseger, who was often depicted as a winged cobra. Meretseger was a cobra-goddess from Thebes whose name meant 'she who loves silence' – presumably the silence of the undisturbed dead. The Egyptians believed that Meretseger lived in the mountains overlooking the Valley of the Kings, an obviously handy vantage point from which to protect the pharaohs buried there. Meretseger had some powerful weapons for that purpose. She could blind anyone caught committing a crime against the pharaohs or inject them with poisonous venom.

PROTECTIVE ANIMALS
The vulture and the cobra

The royal diadem around Tutankhamun's head originally held the images of two creatures which were judged to be symbolically protective in Ancient Egypt. One creature was the Egyptian griffon vulture with outstretched wings, which frequently appeared on Egyptian royal regalia and the ceilings of temples. The same pose was found in a flexible vulture collar found in Tutankamun's tomb: it was inlaid with dark blue, red and green glass. The other image was of a cobra, the sacred representation of Wadjyt, a goddess who was linked to kingship.

MUMMIFYING THE PHARAOH
Shielding the pharaoh's organs

The statue of jackal-headed Duamutef found in the treasury of the tomb of Tutankhamun had the task of protecting the stomach of the dead pharaoh. Duamutef was one of four sons of of Horus, the others were Imsety, Hapy and Qebehsnuef, all of them gods of creation who were born from a lotus flower. It was the task of each son to guard one of Tutankhamun's organs and each was represented bearing a different head. Imsety, who bore a human head, guarded the liver. Hapy, with an ape's head, protected the lungs, and the falcon-headed Qebehsnuef, the intestines. Their combined protection was vital to ensure that Tutankhamun reached the netherworld with a complete body and so could be restored to life.

The Valley of The Kings

In the Valley of the Kings, on the west bank of the Nile, 63 New Kingdom pharaohs were buried with all the splendour that has long been synonymous with the name of Ancient Egypt. Unfortunately, with their fabulous wealth in jewels, gold, silver and other precious metals, and their mass of priceless art objects, the tombs in the Valley have acted as a magnet for robbers, both ancient and modern. The necropolis authorities in charge of the tombs fought back with terrible threats in the form of curses and magic spells and by punishing captured robbers by impaling them on stakes. Even so, the robbers kept coming and still do so today. However, sometimes these robberies were not all they seemed, for the culprits were not just greedy opportunists after loot, but priests and officials who coveted the treasures of the pharaohs for their own purposes. This seamier side of life was, however, mitigated by the technological and scientific achievements of the Ancient Egyptians – their delicate coloured glassware, their skill in fashioning metals, or creating gold imitations and artificial gems. They also possessed great expertise in geometry, mathematics, and other sciences that helped make their civilization one of the most sophisticated in the ancient world.

In the Valley

BURIAL PLACE OF THE PHARAOHS

Between the mountains and the Nile

The Valley of the Kings, where Tutankhamun and 62 other pharaohs were buried, stands on the west bank of the River Nile, some 5 km (3 m) west of Thebes. The first to be buried there was probably Thutmose I (1504–1492 BC), while Rameses XI was the last. There were two valleys. One, the eastern valley, comprised the main royal cemetery; the other, the western, contained the tombs of four pharaohs who reigned after 1390 BC. The double valley is backed by a dramatic range of mountains and some of the royal tombs had to be cut into the rock in a long series of corridors and chambers.

THE SACRED FLOWER OF ANCIENT EGYPT

The meanings of the water lily

Many images of the sacred water lily or lotus were found in the Valley of the Kings. This beautiful flower was revered in Ancient Egypt for its connection with the sun god and the story of creation. This belief came about because the water lily opened at dawn to reveal its brilliant yellow, sun-like centre and closed at night when the Sun set. The water lily was the symbol of Upper Egypt and was frequently found together with the papyrus flower of Lower Egypt, entwined to typify their union.

MOURNING FOR TUTANKHAMUN

Signs of grief

Besides the numerous items packed into the tomb of an Ancient Egyptian pharaoh to see him safely through to the afterlife, there were items left behind that indicated grief at his death. One of these, found in Tutankhamun's tomb, was a floral collar that had been worn by a mourner at his funeral. Nearby was a linen cloth, possibly left behind by another mourner. In some Ancient Egyptian tombs, the entire family of the deceased was pictured in a wall painting, in various poses that indicated grief at their loss.

BOOKS OF THE DEAD

How to manage death

Funerary texts had been introduced in the form of Pyramid texts in the Old Kingdom (*c.* 1000 years earlier than the New Kingdom). The texts in the private tombs were known as the *Book of the Dead* and were written on papyrus. These contained more than 300 different spells, but most papyri only contained a selection. The *Book of the Dead* probably derived from the royal books of the netherworld. One instruction advised the deceased how he should behave to avoid creating 'opposition … in the realm of the dead'. Another describes a test of truthfulness and probity, which the deceased must pass in order to be admitted to the realm of the dead.

SCRIPTS OF ANCIENT EGYPT
Ways to write a book

The Book of the Dead was written in two Ancient Egyptian scripts. One was hieroglyphics or 'sacred carved letters'. Another was hieratic, cursive or 'joined-up' writing. There was a third demotic, popular script, although this was not used for the *Book of the Dead*. A copy of the *Book of the Dead* could be found almost anywhere in a tomb. Some were placed inside the coffin of the deceased, but others were rolled up and inserted into a statuette depicting the gods Sokar and Osiris. Other texts were wrapped up in the bandaging that covered mummified corpses.

LISTING THE PHARAOHS OF ANCIENT EGYPT
Names and deeds

Lists of the pharaohs of Egypt, which could be accompanied by a note of their deeds, were found in several royal temples. Largely, they were accurate, but there were omissions. One was the heretic pharaoh Akhenaten (1352–1336 BC). Quite often, the production of a king list was caused by a pharaoh's need to celebrate royal lineage. Adding his own name to a readymade list allowed him to gain recognition for his right to succeed to the throne. One, dating from around 1300 BC and found in a tomb at Thebes went further: it showed the deceased worshipping the statues of thirteen pharaohs.

Robbers in the Valley

THE TOMB ROBBERS OF ANCIENT EGYPT

Who were the robbers?

Tombs in the Valley of The Kings and elsewhere were looted in ancient times, sometimes soon after the burial. Robberies have continued to this day. However, not all the robbers fitted the popular image of criminals doing their nefarious work under cover of darkness, then sneaking off with their loot. Many of them were the priests or officials who oversaw the construction of a tomb or attended the burial. Some did it for profit, but others entered the tombs to acquire artefacts they wanted for their own burials in the future. Most likely, officials turned a blind eye to what was going on.

WHAT THE ROBBERS WERE LOOKING FOR

The ransacking of the tombs

The opportunistic tomb robber was a messy worker. Most robbers knew what they were looking for. Their chief targets were jewels, gold, metalwork, bedding, oils and unguents and glass. Other marks of the robber were the disorganized state of the tomb after it had been ransacked, the damage sustained by some of the objects, boxes emptied out all over the floor, or unwanted objects casually thrown aside or piled up on top of one another.

CAUGHT IN THE ACT – OR ALMOST

A tomb robber took fright

Tomb robbing in the Valley of the Kings was commonplace and cemeteries were provided with guards who, from time to time, caught robbers in the act. One piece of evidence for this success was a scarf abandoned on the floor of the annexe in Tutankhamun's tomb, presumably when the guards arrived and surprised the robber. Eight gold rings that had scattered over the floor out of the scarf were retrieved, but whether the robber was apprehended or not is unknown.

AN ANCIENT FOOTPRINT

A robber leaves his mark

Tomb robbers were usually in a hurry and left some burial places such as the tomb of Amenhotep III (1390–1352 BC) in a terrible mess. Tutankhamun's tomb was no exception. Despite the belief that it was found intact in 1922, some rooms had been robbed at least twice. Robbers invaded the annexe where the pharaoh's white painted bow box, on the floor, was looted. The thief was in such a rush that he stepped on the box and left his footprint behind, to be found and photographed thousands of years later.

THE ROBBERS' PUNISHMENT
Impaled on a stake

The Ancient Egyptians had a particularly gruesome punishment for robbers who were caught rifling the tombs of the pharaohs. They were impaled on a stake and, apparently, left to die in full public view. This, presumably, was as a warning to others not to commit the same crime. There was a very graphic hieroglyph to express this fearful punishment: a figure impaled at the waist with the rest of his body hanging limply on either side. Doubtless the full weight of his body pressing down on the impaled area increased the agony and was probably meant to.

REPAIRING THE DAMAGE
Resealing a looted tomb

Robberies in the Valley of the Kings were frequent enough for the necropolis authorities to employ restorers to repair the damage and put the tomb back into some sort of order. Some of their work at the tomb of Tutankhamun was less than expert and evidence of robbery was still there when it was found in 1922. The pharaoh's jewellery boxes were discovered, their contents scattered over the floor and the restorers failed to reseal any of the boxes. But the breaches the robbers had made in the walls to get into the antechamber were repaired and plastered over. The work was stamped with the necropolis seal – a jackal surmounting nine bound prisoners.

Good Luck, Bad Luck

HEADING OFF DISASTER
Amulets as protection against evil

Ancient Egyptian society was deeply superstitious and all classes were conscious of evil, bad luck and other misfortunes and what they could do to obtain protection. This was why amulets and similar charms were so frequently worn. Besides the task of protecting their wearers, amulets may have signified the hope that they would acquire certain virtues or advantages, such as the strength of a bull or the courage of a lion. Amulets could be made from several different materials – metal, glass, stone or faïence (*see* page 94), all of which were thought to have magical properties.

HORUS TO THE RESCUE
Protection from dangerous animals

The Ancient Egyptians recruited the sky god, Horus, to shield them from dangerous animals such as the crocodiles or hippopotami who lived in and around the River Nile, or from scorpions and snakes. Among the more popular amulets or stele – slabs of wood or stone carrying inscriptions – were those that bore an image of the sky god Horus as a child. He was shown standing on the back of a crocodile, with snakes and scorpions in his arms. The purpose of this image was to provide powers of healing against their bites and stings.

LUCKY DAYS, UNLUCKY DAYS

A special calendar

Ancient Egyptian calendars featured good days and bad days. One calendar, presently at the British Museum in London, marks the good days in black and the bad days in red – red for danger, perhaps. Each day's entry carried three hieroglyphs indicating 'lucky' or 'unlucky. For a 'bad' day, there might be an instruction not to leave the house, not to work at sunset or, more chillingly, the prediction that anyone born on this day would die by a serpent bite. A 'good' day, on the other hand, would carry the legend, 'This is the day the gods received their hearts. The world observes a festival.'

SPELLS AND CURSES
Frightening predictions

Curses and spells had great influence in Ancient Egypt, for popular superstitions gave them great power. Curses could be found in tombs, or on stele or statues. For example, this warning was inscribed in hieroglyphics at the entrance to the tomb of a minor official named Petety, buried at the Cemetery of the Artisans near Giza: 'Listen, all of you!' the warning read. 'The priest of Hathor [an important cow goddess] will beat twice any one of you who enters this tomb or does harm to it ... [If] anyone … does anything bad to my tomb, then the crocodile, hippopotamus and the lion will eat him.'

CURSES IN THE TOMBS
Even more frightening predictions

The curse of Petety was mild compared with some of those inscribed in tombs and temples, stele, statues and at times inside coffins. 'He shall be cooked together with the condemned' was inscribed on one 18th-Dynasty tomb. 'His lifetime shall not exist on earth' was another 18th-Dynasty curse. But worse than any of these was: 'A donkey shall violate him, a donkey shall violate his wife,' one of several graffiti from a 20th-Dynasty tomb.

ASTROLOGY IN ANCIENT EGYPT
The pharaoh's signs of the zodiac

Signs of the zodiac used in Ancient Egypt had a form familiar to modern devotees of horoscopes. The year was divided into twelve astrological months and a god or goddess was assigned to each. Each month accorded virtues and strengths to those born under its sign. The year began on 29 August with Thoth, the god of learning, as guardian over the subsequent month. It was completed on the following 28 August – August being the month of Anubis, guardian of the netherworld.

The Sciences in Ancient Egypt

ANCIENT EGYPTIAN ASTRONOMY
Reading the sky

To the Ancient Egyptians, astronomy was part of their religion and funerary practices. Ceilings of temples, tombs and coffins were decorated with pictures of the sun and stars. In this, religion was mixed with science. By about 1850 BC, Egyptian astronomers had discovered five of the eight planets in the solar system apart from Earth. But all five, termed 'stars that know no rest', were conceived as deities sailing across the heavens in barks.

MATHEMATICS
The Ancient Egyptian numbers system

The Ancient Egyptians had no individual numbers, but instead used hieroglyphic 'letters' for mathematical purposes. 'Numbers' were written from right to left, starting with the largest figure. This 'additive' numbers system was used for measuring the level of the Nile inundations, reckoning areas of land, calculating taxes and time and counting money and the days of the year. The Egyptians came closer than any other ancient civilization to the true length of the solar year – they were 'out' by only six hours.

HOW THE TOMBS WERE BUILT

An unchanging enterprise

Egyptian tombs were almost always built underground and consisted of a simple pit, and a room or rooms cut out of the subterranean rock or a chamber made of mud-brick or stone. The most important area, though, was not the actual burial place of the deceased. Rather, tomb architects concentrated on the funerary chapel. They installed statues of the deceased, stele describing him or her and provided special areas where offerings could be made to the gods. These facilities ensured that the dead would be accepted into the afterlife.

The Valley of The Kings

BUILDING A PYRAMID
The pyramids at Giza

The most famous of Ancient Egyptian pyramid tombs, as well as the most visible, are the pyramids at Giza, which lie on the west bank of the Nile opposite Cairo and comprise the only surviving Wonder of the Ancient World. The Giza structures were built with three burial chambers instead of the usual one and included shafts that accessed the open air above. It has been suggested that these had an astronomical purpose, since the pyramids seem to have been deliberately aligned with the constellation of Orion.

THE TRADE OF ANCIENT EGYPT

Trading by barter

Money as presently understood was virtually unknown in Egypt and the ancient Middle East, where trading was done by barter. To ensure fair trading, barter goods had their set values, which was expressed in numbers of copper deben. This system operated in both domestic and foreign trade, though trade outside Egypt was usually dressed up in diplomatic missions carrying luxury cargo as tribute. Many of the paintings found in tombs of the 18th Dynasty showed scenes in which trade goods were presented to foreign rulers as 'gifts'. They were more than that: often, 'gifts' comprised gold statues that had been specially requested from the 'buyers'.

DOWN TO THE SEA

The ships of Ancient Egypt

The all-pervading presence of the River Nile made travel by water a natural recourse in Ancient Egypt. Ships and boats were also tied up with burial practices, for models of them were placed in tombs. The sun god Ra was frequently depicted travelling across the sky or, at night, through the netherworld in a solar bark. Reeds from the Nile provided a natural material for ship and boat construction. Vessels could be quite substantial, with upturned prows and sterns, large steering oars, several rowing oars and a number of crew. Some ships were provided with long, narrow sails and even a cabin for shelter from the sun.

Putting the Sciences to Work

SCIENCE AND TECHNOLOGY
Inventions and innovations

Inevitably, because of its great antiquity, the technology of Ancient Egypt was low- rather than high-tech. Within that limitation, though, Egyptian achievement was impressive. They used papyrus from the Nile delta to make paper and invented aids for construction, such as the lever and the ramp. They built the first monumental stone buildings, using stone, copper or bronze tools. They were the first to use stern-mounted rudders on ships, rather than quarter-rudders mounted on the sides and had an important influence on the development of lighthouses.

ANCIENT EGYPTIAN METALLURGY
Mixing metals

The Egyptians had a considerable working knowledge of metallurgy, with skills in extracting copper from ores mined in the desert between the Nile and the Red Sea. Later, they worked in iron, which they called 'the metal of Heaven' because of the occasional meteorite which brought iron to Earth from space. The Egyptians also employed a case-hardening process that sharpened the edges of iron tools and used tin in the manufacture of bronze, and cobalt for colouring glass.

GOLD
Extracting gold in Ancient Egypt

The Ancient Egyptian word for gold was *nub*, after the land of Nubia south of Egypt, where it was mined in large quantities. Gold mining was a major undertaking, employing hundreds of workers. As many as 1,300 gold miners' houses have been found close to the Red Sea. The Egyptians also 'panned' gold from the alluvia of rivers. To extract the metal, gold-bearing sand was poured into a bag made of a fleece with the wool on the inside. After being vigorously shaken, the water was poured away, taking the earth with it and the gold was left clinging to the wool.

ANCIENT EGYPTIAN CHEMISTRY
Chemical recipes

Ancient Egyptian chemists have long been recognized as the pioneers of their science and several manuscripts detailing their knowledge have been found by archaeologists. One of them, the Leyden Papyrus, comprised a collection of some 75 chemical recipes and directions for making metal alloys and imitations of gold, silver or electrum, dyeing textiles and soldering metals. Another manuscript, the Stockholm Papyrus, detailed 70 recipes for producing artificial gems and another ten for whitening off-colour pearls. Purifying tin, whitening copper with arsenic and preparing chrysocolla, a solder for gold, were also among the contents.

ANCIENT EGYPTIAN GEOMETRY

Measuring by geometry

A knowledge of geometry existed early on in the history of Ancient Egypt. Egyptian geometers knew, for example, that the area of a rectangle equalled its length multiplied by its width. And that if they drew a triangle inside the rectangle with the same length as its sides and the same height as its width, then the area of the triangle was half the area of the rectangle. A major achievement of Ancient Egyptian geometry was using the diameter of a circle to calculate its area. With this knowledge, they were also able to calculate volume.

ANCIENT EGYPTIAN MEDICINE

Magic and science

Some doctors in Ancient Egypt resorted to curing disease or injury by magic spells, amulets and religious incantations. Others appear to have followed a more practical, scientific approach from quite early on. As far back as the Third Dynasty (2686–2613 BC), surgeons, veterinary surgeons and dentists were at work and several medical papyri have been found by archaeologists. These indicate a knowledge of anatomy and the role of the pulse in diagnosing heart conditions. One papyrus listed treatments for broken or dislocated bones and crush injuries. Another specialized in stomach complaints, gynaecological complaints and skin irritations.

Egypt and The Nile

In the fifth century BC, when the Ancient Greek historian Herodotus described Egypt as the 'gift of the Nile', he hit the nail right on the head. The Nile was so all-pervading that it was, in itself, responsible for the very existence of Ancient Egypt. Beyond the river were desert and scrubland. But where the river ran there was a metamorphosis. As it flowed through the narrow ribbon of land that crossed the wilderness, the Nile made it possible to grow fruits, vegetables and plants in fertile profusion. It became home to an extraordinary variety of wild life – from crocodiles, snakes and hippopotami to birds, frogs, scorpions and other insects, as well as the cattle, sheep, goats and other animals that worked on the Nile farms. As a waterway, the Nile acted as a conduit for travel and communications. The traditional felucca, which plied the river in ancient times can still be seen there now. Evidence of Ancient Egyptian civilization that has lasted for thousands of years can still be seen close to the Nile – magnificent temples, the pyramids of Giza or the Great Sphinx, whose identity and purpose are still the subject of debate and speculation today.

The Gift of the Nile

THE SOURCE OF EGYPT'S CIVILIZATION
The world's longest river

At 6,695 km (4,160 m) the River Nile is the longest river in the world and could also be called the world's longest oasis. For this ribbon of water flowing through desert and scrubland, deep canyons and high plateaux, was the reason for the existence of Ancient Egypt and its splendid civilization. Or, as the Greek historian Herodotus (485–425 BC) put it after he visited Egypt in around 445 BC: 'The Nile is the gift of [the god] Osiris, but Egypt is the gift of the Nile.'

THE INUNDATION
The fertilizing river

Herodotus also wrote that every year, 'The river rises of itself, waters the fields, and then sinks back again; thereupon each man sows his field and waits for the harvest.' It sounds miraculous, but as long as the waters washing down the Nile from Khartoum in the Sudan kept to its schedule, it was true. The secret of the Inundation, as the Egyptians called it, was the exceptionally fertile mud that the Nile deposited on its banks between June and September. It was the perfect fertilizer and in some years, made it possible to grow two crops in a single year.

GODS OF THE INUNDATION
Hapy and Osiris

Hapy, Egyptian god of the Inundation, was one of the four sons of Horus and a grandson of Osiris. Osiris himself was the god of fertility among other roles, and overseeing the fertility the Inundation brought to Egypt was an important function. Hapy was usually represented as a well-fed middle-aged man, the very picture of contentment. He was fat, with a pot belly, and his role as god of the Inundation was emphasized by his headdress of aquatic plants.

THE NILOMETER
Measuring the inundation

The nilometer looked like an ordinary staircase, or series of rough steps, leading up from the bank of the Nile to the fertile fields beyond, but it had a particularly vital function. The nilometer was a measuring instrument, designed to show the height of the Nile waters that flooded the fields during the Inundation. Some ancient nilometers have survived. The best known is on Elephantine Island at Aswan, which was rebuilt by the Romans when they ruled Egypt after 30 BC.

WHITE NILE, BLUE NILE
Two rivers make one

Strictly speaking, the Nile is not one river, but three. One is the so-called White Nile, which flows from Lake Victoria Nyanza, the largest lake in Africa, covering parts of present-day Kenya, Uganda and Tanzania. At Khartoum, in the Sudan, the White Nile joins the Blue and so becomes the River Nile, which is joined in Sudan by the third river, the Atbara. The combined river continues over a series of cataracts until it reaches the Mediterranean Sea at Alexandria. The Blue Nile is said to flow to its confluence with the White Nile from from, among other sources, a sacred spring at Gishe Abbai, 1,800 metres up in the Ethiopian mountains.

THE NILE REACHES THE SEA
The Nile Delta

The delta of the River Nile is so extensive that it occupies more than three fifths of the inhabited area of Egypt. Its two branches cover around 80,000 sq km (49,700 sq m) and are fringed by lakes, lagoons, wetlands and sand dunes. The papyrus, Ancient Egypt's most versatile plant, has long grown in profusion. The delta has mythical connotations. Its 'islands', 12 metres high and made of sand and clay, were thought to indicate that creation itself began on a mound of earth. This took place in the primordial waters of Nun, the god who personified the ocean that preceded the advent of the sun god Amun.

Living by the Nile

PHARAOHS AND THE NILE
Pharaohs hunting

Hunting, fishing and fowling were frequent sports of pharaohs and their courtiers. These, though, were not simply for entertainment but also had ritual and religious significance. Hunting scenes as depicted on the walls of tombs and temples served to emphasize a pharaoh's courage and prowess. They also underlined his dominance over the creatures of his realm. One ritualized scene showed Tutankhamun hunting birds in the Nile marshes with a vulture, representing kingship, hovering above his head and the birds, which were his prey, representing the enemies of the gods.

A VARIETY OF PREY
Choose your weapon

The fertility of Ancient Egypt supported a large variety of animals in and around the River Nile. For hunting, the pharaohs had plenty to choose from, varying from small, easy prey such as rabbits and birds to more challenging creatures like elephants and lions (although these latter they hunted on their foreign campaigns to Palestine and Syria, keeping them in hunting parks, as they had died out due to climatic changes in Egypt before dynastic times). Deer, gazelles, oryx, antelopes, hippopotami, crocodiles and bulls also featured among the many wild animals hunted by the pharaohs. Weapons that could be used from a safe distance were the obvious choice for hunting and at least four were readily available: the bow and arrow, the slingstone, throwstick and spear.

FISHING IN THE RIVER NILE
The poor man's sport and sustenance

Apart from sport, the hunt provided skins and meat but only for those who could afford it. Poorer Egyptians, who could not, found a handy substitute in fishing the Nile. For this they used the basic hook and line, harpoons, traps and nets. There were numerous species of fish in the river and the marshes of the delta and beyond that, the Mediterranean Sea. Birds were fortunately within a poor man's budget and there was a plentiful supply of geese and ducks in the marshes and the papyrus thickets that grew beside the Nile.

JEWELS OF THE NILE I
The temples at Karnak

The Karnak temple complex was a 'work in progress' throughout virtually the entire history of Ancient Egyptian civilization. Successive pharaohs extended, altered and decorated its buildings from at least around 2055 BC and were still doing so after the Romans arrived in 30 BC. The Karnak site covered over one hundred hectares, and comprised three huge precincts dedicated to the sun god Amun, the vulture goddess Mut and Montu, the falcon-headed god of war. Of these the most elaborate was the temple of Amun, which contained several courtyards, obelisks, shrines, altars and smaller temples.

JEWELS OF THE NILE II
The rock temples of Abu Simbel

The two rock temples of Abu Simbel, fronted by giant statues of Rameses II (1279–1213 BC), were rescued from destruction in 1971 after the building of the Aswan High Dam threatened to submerge them. The temples were dismantled and moved to a higher location. On their original site, they were carefully aligned so that twice a year, in February and October, the rays of the rising sun would penetrate into the cavernous interior which had been cut deep inside the rock wall.

JEWELS OF THE NILE III
The Great Sphinx of Giza

The Great Sphinx of Giza is the most famous example of a frequently sculpted figure from Ancient Egypt – a mythical beast with the head of a man and the body of a lion. The head of the Great Sphinx is thought to represent Pharaoh Khafra (2558–2535 BC), who was buried in the second pyramid at Giza, which is sited nearby. The Great Sphinx has frequently been subject to erosion, and has lost both its nose and beard. In addition, it has long been in danger from its desert environment. The Sphinx has been submerged in sand – and subsequently rescued from it – on several occasions.

Working by the Nile

THE INFLUENCE OF THE NILE

The Nile as symbol

The River Nile as an entity symbolized almost every area of Ancient Egyptian life. Ra, the sun god was thought to use a ferry to travel across the sky every day. The hippopotamus whose shape made it appear perpetually pregnant, was adopted for representations of Tawaret, goddess of women in childbirth. Hequet, the frog, or Sobek, the crocodile, were also revered for their role in childbirth and fertility. River plants such as the water lily and papyrus were frequently used in hieroglyphs and other writings and had an 'heraldic' purpose as symbols, respectively, of Upper and Lower Egypt. And in architecture, the waves of the Nile were used as decoration on walls and columns.

LANDOWNERS AND PEASANTS
Missing the quota

In Ancient Egypt, as in many other realms, the land was not owned by the people who farmed it. Instead, it was the property of the pharaoh, or the priests of the temple who kept very strict records of what was produced. Farmers were allowed to keep a portion of the crops for themselves and their families but they had to meet the assigned grain quotas, which were a type of taxation. However, there were dire punishments for farmers and farm workers who failed to achieve their quotas. Some of the Ancient Egyptian tombs have paintings of scenes in which farmers were beaten for failing to provide sufficient grain, as agreed beforehand.

FARMING IN ANCIENT EGYPT
The three seasons

For farmers, the working year was divided into three seasons. The first was Akhet, the Inundation which saw the annual flooding of the Nile. Next came Peret, the growing season when the ploughing and planting was done. Finally, it was time for Shemu, or harvesting, when the crops were cut and stored. This routine involved plenty of time during which farmers and their workers had little to do, as they waited first for the Inundation to finish, the Nile waters to recede and, finally, the crops to grow. This time was not wasted, however. During these 'idle' periods, farmers worked on construction and other public projects.

THE TOOLS FOR THE JOB
Farming implements in Ancient Egypt

Almost every activity possible was depicted in the wall paintings of Ancient Egyptian tombs and the hard work involved in farming by the Nile was no exception. The paintings show how grain was harvested with sickle and threshing was done using oxen as the motive power. Winnowing and storing the grain came next. Ancient Egypt was a bureaucratic society. At all stages, scribes were there, meticulously measuring and recording how much grain had been produced before it was stored away.

AN ANCIENT CLASSIC
The shaduf

One of the world's most long-lasting tools is the shaduf, for which evidence exists on an Akkadian cylinder seal dated around 4,000 years ago. It was introduced into Egypt around 1,000 years later, during the 18th Dynasty. This simple but extremely effective low-tech tool was used to irrigate the land. The shaduf comprised a long wooden pole with a bowl or bucket at one end and a counterbalancing weight at the other. The bowl was immersed in the Nile or an irrigation canal, swivelled landward and then emptied over the soil. Much later, the shaduf was replaced as a means of raising water by the Archimedes Screw and the water wheel. Even so, the shaduf can still be seen at work along the River Nile today.

MAXIMIZING THE NILE FLOODS
Irrigation on the Nile

The great boon of Ancient Egypt, the annual inundatilon of the Nile, was maximized by irrigation. Farmers waited until mid-August, when the floods had reached their maximum depth and the waters began to subside. They then set about digging irrigation canals and blocking them so that the water was retained. This greatly extended the reach of the Nile and also enabled farmers to transfer the water to places where the level was low. The flood water was released in the fields about six weeks later.

Animals of the Nile

THE NILE HIPPOPOTAMUS
Protector or destroyer

The hippopotamus disappeared from the River Nile some time after the pharaohs of the 18th Dynasty ruled in Ancient Egypt. While it was still there, however, the male of the species at least was regarded as a danger. While females were revered and the hippopotamus goddess Tawaret was revered for her protective role in childbirth, the males were seen as destructive evil-doers. They trampled growing crops or ate them and made themselves such a nuisance that even children at school were warned against them together with another culprit, the worm: 'The worm has taken half the grain,' ran one New Kingdom school text book, 'the hippopotamus has devoured the rest.' Hippopotamus hunts designed to reduce the population were already being organized in Egypt in prehistoric times.

THE NILE CROCODILES I
Fearing the crocodile

The Nile crocodile was not only a danger lying silently in wait on the banks of the river, but it lurked in the water itself, easily overturning the light papyrus craft that plied the river. Crocodiles also attacked herds of animals fording the Nile, although in the hope of diverting them, their driver uttered a special spell all the way across. It was little comfort that the other scourge of the river, the hippopotamus, could be bitten in half by a crocodile. Yet, though crocodiles were rightly regarded with fear, some, according to the Greek historian Herodotus, were kept as pampered pets.

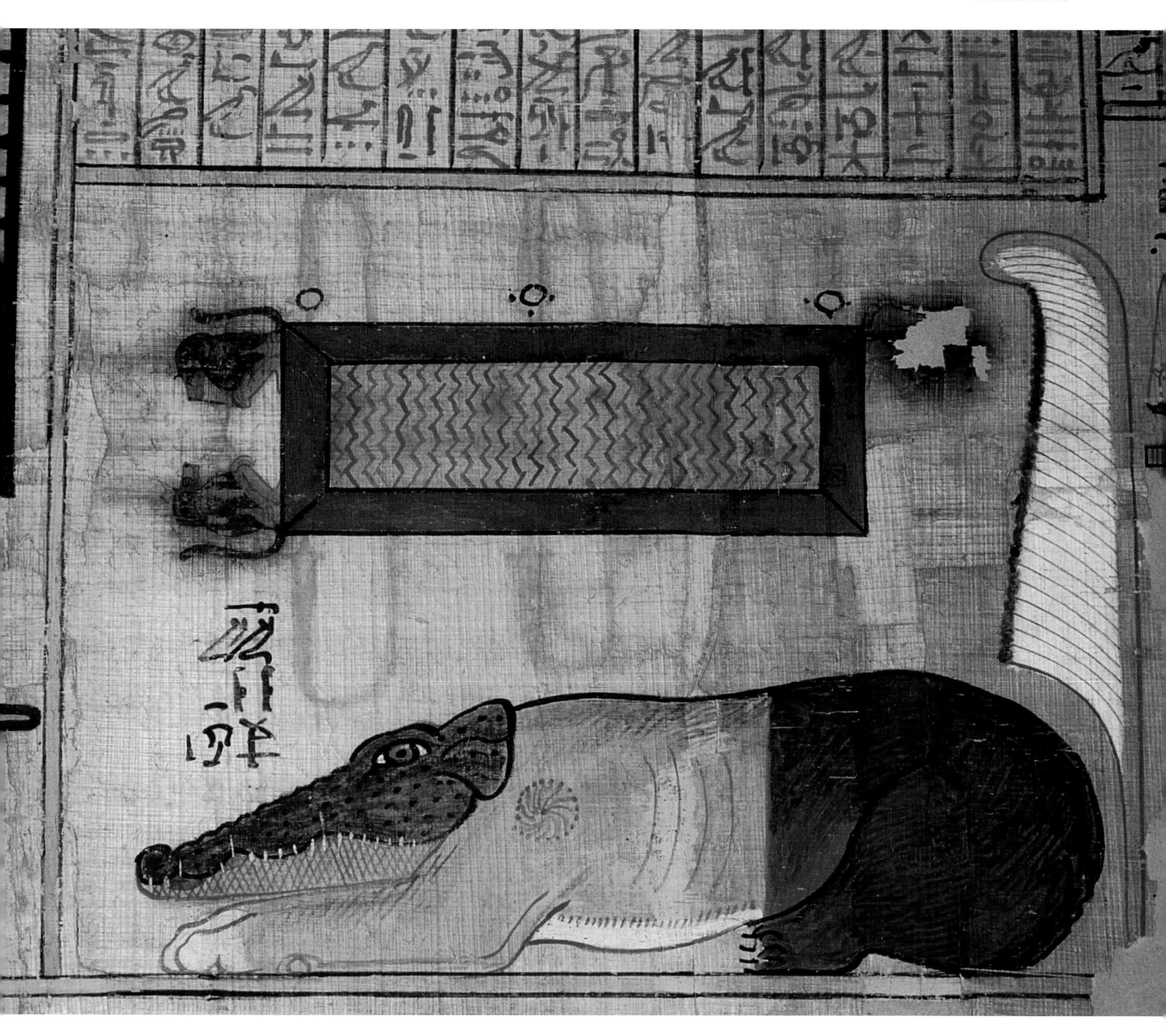

THE NILE CROCODILES II
Worshipping a crocodile

Some crocodiles were revered for their strength and fearlessness. One such reptile who enjoyed remarkable privileges was kept in a pool at Crocodilopolis, the centre in western Egypt, where worship of the crocodile god Sobek took place. This creature was pampered to an extreme: it was regularly fed, decked out in expensive jewellery and worshipped by members of the cult. Other shrines and temples dedicated to Sobek were found throughout the Nile Valley. Dead crocodiles were discovered in their own sarcophagi, embalmed and mummified, sometimes together with crocodile eggs.

ANIMALS AT WORK
Farming animals

Ancient Egyptian farmers used most of the animals historically connected with agriculture. Oxen were harnessed to the plough, cattle, sheep, pigs and goats were raised to supply meat. Flocks of geese, ducks or pigeons were also kept for this purpose and in addition supplied farmers with eggs. Donkeys served as pack animals and were particularly evident early on in Ancient Egypt: ten donkey skeletons were found in the tomb of the second pharaoh, Aha (*c.* 3100 BC), when it was excavated by Flinders Petrie from 1899 to 1900.

CAT WORSHIP IN ANCIENT EGYPT
Cats as symbols of the divine

Cats occupied an extraordinary position in Ancient Egypt as symbols of deities. One was the sun god Ra, who was represented in the form of 'the great cat of Heliopolis', another was the cat-goddess Bastet, who was regarded as Ra's daughter. The earliest depiction of cats took the form of three hieroglyphic symbols that showed them seated and partly formed the description 'Lord of the City of the Cats'. Cat images frequently appeared in tomb paintings, participating in hunting scenes or fowling in the Nile marshes, and simply seated under their owners' chairs. Cats were less passive when appearing in the funerary texts where they were shown as demons beheading bound prisoners.

SERPENTS AND SCORPIONS OF THE NILE
Powers of evil and protection

Both serpents and scorpions were the objects of cult worship but also the subjects of spells to counteract the dangers they represented. Both had their special deities. In the case of scorpions it was the goddess Serket or Selket, who was usually depicted with a scorpion on her head. There was also a less well-known god associated with the scorpion – Shed, frequently described as 'the Saviour'. The prinicipal benefit offered by Serket and Shed was protection from the scorpion's deadly sting. Snakes, which could proliferate around the River Nile, were likewise feared for their poisonous bites but their chief deity, Wadjyt, had an honourable place in Ancient Egypt as the patroness of Lower Egypt and a symbol of the power of the pharaohs.

Travelling the Nile

BOATS ON THE NILE

The barge of the sun

The concept of a solar barge derived from prehistoric times and came down to the Ancient Egyptians as a symbol of the sun's daily journey across the sky. There are many depictions of the sun god Ra and later Horus 'sailing' in the barge through an underground channel from west to east before emerging as the rising sun. Models of the barge were found in the tomb of Khufu (2589–2566 BC) inside the Great Pyramid of Giza. This ship was a life-size example, just over 43 m (141 ft) long, and is the oldest boat found by archaeologists.

FUNERARY BOATS ON THE NILE
Last journey along the river

At some funerals in Ancient Egypt, funerary boats were used to take the deceased along the Nile in imitation of the Sun god's journey in his solar barge. According to Ancient Egyptian belief, the sun took the soul of a dead man or woman on its voyage to the 'upper waters' or the heavens. To facilitate this journey a real or model boat, usually resembling the real-life papyrus boats that sailed the Nile, was placed in every tomb.

THE NILE WIND
Sailing directions

Successfully navigating the Nile meant understanding the way the wind blew along the river. In the Nile valley, the prevailing wind came from the north. Boats travelling south could fill their sails with the wind and move smoothly through the water. Boats voyaging north, against the wind, had to rely on their oars and the river current. Ancient Egyptian hieroglyphs expressed this difference with a sign showing a northbound boat with its sails down, while 'travelling south' was shown by a boat with sails billowing in the wind.

SAILING THE NILE YESTERDAY AND TODAY

The felucca

The felucca, with its distinctive triangular lateen sail, is a traditional boat still seen on the Nile today. Feluccas have provided transport on the river since ancient times. In keeping with tradition, today's feluccas still move along the Nile by means of the river current and the Nile breeze, which builds up as the day goes on but subsides at night. Feluccas do not carry keels, but there is a form of substitute – a heavy centreplate that can be raised clear of the riverbed when the boat enters the shallows.

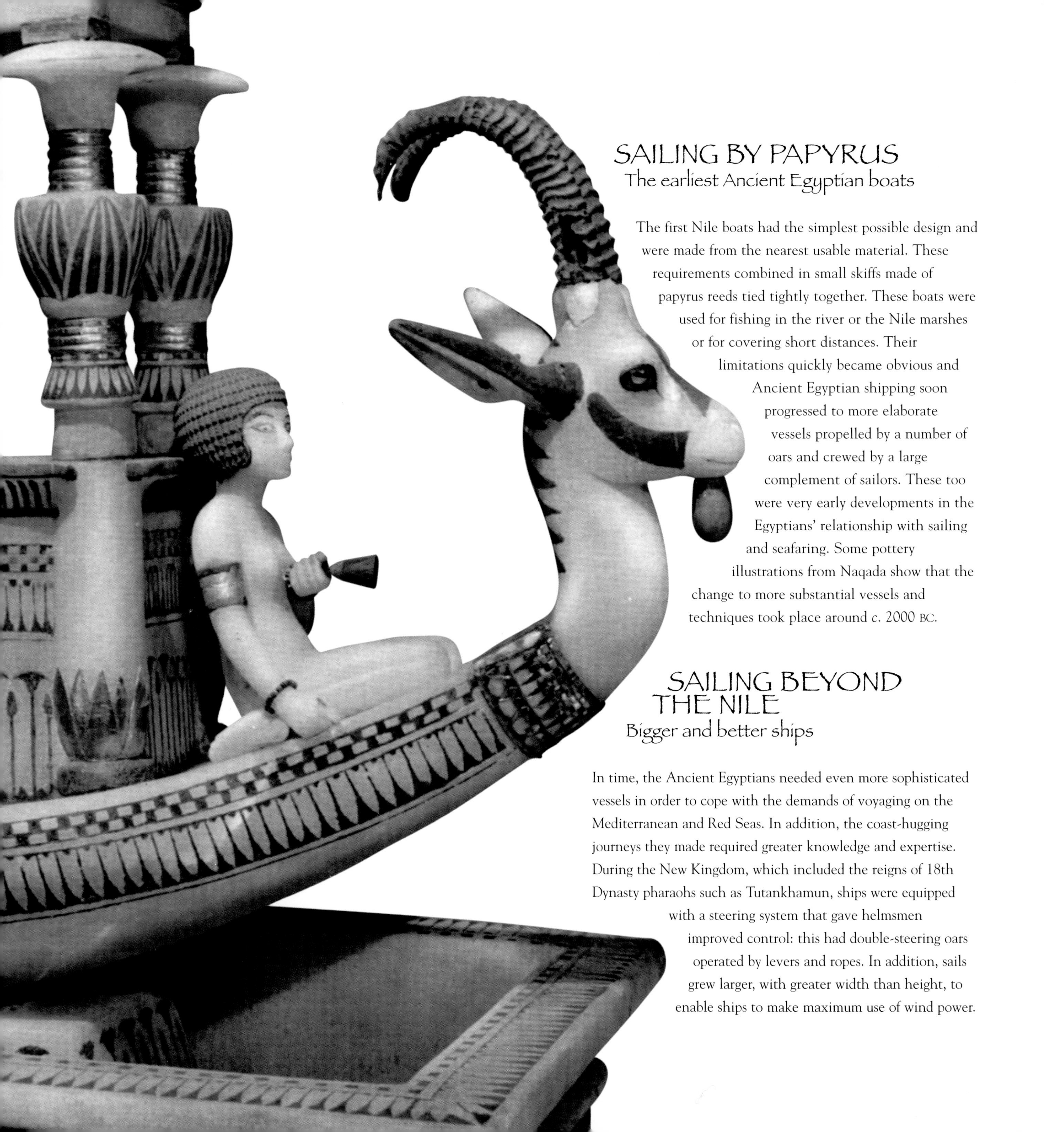

SAILING BY PAPYRUS

The earliest Ancient Egyptian boats

The first Nile boats had the simplest possible design and were made from the nearest usable material. These requirements combined in small skiffs made of papyrus reeds tied tightly together. These boats were used for fishing in the river or the Nile marshes or for covering short distances. Their limitations quickly became obvious and Ancient Egyptian shipping soon progressed to more elaborate vessels propelled by a number of oars and crewed by a large complement of sailors. These too were very early developments in the Egyptians' relationship with sailing and seafaring. Some pottery illustrations from Naqada show that the change to more substantial vessels and techniques took place around *c.* 2000 BC.

SAILING BEYOND THE NILE

Bigger and better ships

In time, the Ancient Egyptians needed even more sophisticated vessels in order to cope with the demands of voyaging on the Mediterranean and Red Seas. In addition, the coast-hugging journeys they made required greater knowledge and expertise. During the New Kingdom, which included the reigns of 18th Dynasty pharaohs such as Tutankhamun, ships were equipped with a steering system that gave helmsmen improved control: this had double-steering oars operated by levers and ropes. In addition, sails grew larger, with greater width than height, to enable ships to make maximum use of wind power.

Upper Egypt and Lower Egypt

The Ancient Egyptian empire that saw the rise to power of the 18th Dynasty was the first of its kind to emerge in the Middle East. It gave the pharaohs – the young though ill-fated Tutankhamun among them – control over territory stretching as far south as Nubia, a rich source of gold, and eastwards to the river Euphrates in Mesopotamia. The Egyptian conquests also extended westwards into the desert and scrubland between the river Nile and Libya and to the northeast into Palestine and Syria.

The force that conquered this huge expanse of territory was Egypt's first permanent army, which was directed by a tightly disciplined officer corps with the pharaoh himself as supreme commander. But the Ancient Egyptians were not too proud to ignore the lessons of their own previous defeats. They borrowed judiciously from enemies who had once invaded and overrun Egypt, by adopting the horse-drawn chariot and composite bow developed by the Hyksos and the double bow used by the Hittites.

As a result, the Egyptians were able to initiate a period of dominance – political, geographical and financial – that lasted some two centuries and gave a boost to Egypt's already impressive record of technical, cultural and scientific achievement.

The Growing Power of Egypt

THE EMPIRE OF ANCIENT EGYPT

The beginnings of empire

The Ancient Egyptian empire began, paradoxically, with a foreign invasion that completely overran the country and put it under foreign rule for more than a century. The invaders were the Hyksos, a Semitic people from Palestine who first entered Egypt by way of the Nile delta and extended their power southwards from there. Their leaders set themselves up as pharaohs and brutally suppressed any Egyptian uprisings. Ultimately, after two centuries, in around 1600 BC, a leader arose with the drive and charisma that were needed to expel the intruders.

REVOLT IN THEBES

Expelling the Hyksos

Some time after 1600 BC a revolt against the Hyksos, brewed in Thebes by Egyptian nobles, finally succeeded where so many others had failed. The rebels seemed to have chosen their time well, for fighting between rival heirs to the throne of the childless Hyksos pharaoh Aauserra Apepi II (1585–1542 BC) weakened royal and government authority and initiated their collapse. Too weak to resist the rebel onslaught, the Hyksos were driven out of Upper Egypt and pushed back all the way to Palestine.

BACK IN POWER

Egyptian military muscle

The central figure in this success was the Pharaoh Ahmose I (1550–1525 BC), the first ruler of the 18th Dynasty of Ancient Egypt. Ahmose was not content to rest on his laurels after he sent the Hyksos packing. His ambitions were greater than that. But he understood that Egypt had to become a first-class military power before those ambitions could be realized. Ahmose began by creating Egypt's first permanent army and, as its backbone, a body of well-trained, disciplined archers.

STRENGTHENING THE PHARAOH'S POWER

Introducing the chariot

One of the advantages the Hyksos had enjoyed in war with Egypt had been the chariot, which could carry archers, spearmen and other soldiers round a battlefield at high speed and slaughter infantry with terrifying efficiency. Ahmose had probably witnessed what the chariot could do and how troops could be demoralized by it. He added it to his weaponry and made sure he had a corps of charioteers skilful enough to maximize its potential. He also dispensed with a cardinal weakness in former Egyptian governments – the autonomy that had allowed provincial nobles to wield too much power. Ahmose neutralized these local strong men by centralizing the government under his own control.

CONQUERING AN EMPIRE
The warrior pharaohs

The first campaign of conquest conducted by Ahmose I was against the Hyksos. Nubia, south of Egypt and bordering the Red Sea, was an important asset, since it acted as a corridor for lucrative trade between tropical Africa and the Mediterranean. The successors of Ahmose, Amenhotep I (1525–1504 BC) and Thutmose I (1504–1492 BC) continued his work, extending Egyptian rule westwards into Libya, and north-eastwards into Palestine and Syria. The Egyptian army advanced so far into Mesopotamia that it reached the banks of the River Euphrates.

THE HEIGHT OF EGYPTIAN POWER
The Battle of Megiddo, 1469 BC

The showdown that finally elevated Egypt to superpower status took place at the Battle of Megiddo, the first battle ever recorded, in 1469 BC. The combatants were Thutmose III (1479–1425 BC), grandson of the first Thutmose, and rebellious chieftains who thought they could exploit the pharaoh's youth and inexperience. They were mistaken. Thutmose, leading an army 10,000 strong, pushed through the Megiddo Pass, which had been heavily defended by the rebels, and enveloped them near the fortress of Megiddo. After this victory, Egyptian rule was extended deep into Asia Minor and north-western Mesopotamia. What was more, the Egyptian fleet controlled the eastern Mediterranean.

At the Pharaoh's Command

EGYPT SUPREME
Two centuries of dominance

Megiddo was a seminal military victory that changed the history of Egypt for some two centuries – from a land under foreign pressure to a state triumphant over its enemies. More invasions, more foreign conquests and finally, in the twelfth century BC, the start of irreversible decline lay in its future, but by the time Tutankhamun became Pharaoh in around 1336 BC, he was the ruler of a powerful, successful state able to call most, if not all, of the shots in the Middle East. As such, the youthful Tutunkhamun was depicted as a mighty warrior pharaoh, like his illustrious predecessors.

THE MIGHTY PHARAOH
Tutankhamun as a war leader

It is unlikely that Tutankhamun ever led his troops into battle. Nevertheless, he was frequently depicted as a successful war leader. One of his military images was provided by the blue war crown, a tall helmet decorated with golden disks, a cobra and a vulture, which first appeared in the 18th Dynasty. On a triangular gold fragment found in his tomb, Tutankhamun was shown wearing this crown while holding a fallen enemy by the hair with one hand and a large mace in the other.

THE FORCES OF ANCIENT EGYPT

The world's first standing army

In the army of Ancient Egypt, the pharaoh occupied his natural place as supreme commander. Below him was his commander of the army, then four generals chosen from royal princes or favourites and senior court officials. The role of the generals was advisory rather than military. Next in the military hierarchy were senior officers who acted as commanders and after them the platoon leaders, who were the equivalent of modern non-commissioned officers such as sergeants. The army was divided into four divisions, which were named after Ancient Egyptian gods – Amun, Ptah, Seth and the sun god Ra.

CAPTIVES OF THE PHARAOH
Depicting the defeated

The Egyptians usually depicted a defeated enemy as a tied and helpless captive. Images of a Nubian and an Asian tightly bound to a staff were found in Tutankhamun's tomb and another black Nubian was tied to a stick with a curved end. A variation on this theme, from the tomb of Rameses II (1279–1213 BC) was a painting showing the pharaoh trampling Bedouin tribesmen underfoot, probably during the campaigns to extend the Pharaoh's power over the desert west of Egypt.

MERCENARIES
The Sherden pirates

The most ferocious fighters among the numerous mercenaries who served in the Ancient Egyptian army were the Sherden, who came from Turkey and had a fearsome reputation as pirates. Their prey were vessels that ventured too far out for safety into the Mediterranean. Rameses II (1279–1213 BC) defeated the Sherden, but realizing their military prowess, recruited them into his army. The Sherden carried distinctive straight swords and wore protective helmets with horns attached, doubtless to make them look even more ferocious than they were. The Sherden fought for Rameses against the Hittites in the battle of Qadesh (1294 BC) and appeared on a commemorative relief at the temple of Abydos.

JOBS IN HIGH PLACES

The senior ranks

Although a scribe or other educated Egyptian could rise up the ranks to high command, most army officers came from the aristocracy. These officers needed to be well educated as well as skilled strategists and able leaders, but to cement their loyalty, pharaohs lavished upon them splendid gifts of land, gold or slaves. The greatest gifts of all were the prestigious titles which only pharaohs were able to bestow – archery commander, divisional commander, commander of the chariot corps or most important of all, overseer of the royal stables.

Conquering an Empire

ANCIENT EGYPT AT WAR
Learning from the enemy

Initially, the army of Ancient Egypt was not equipped with sophisticated weapons. The light infantry carried a basic curved bow and bronze-tipped arrows. The heavy infantry were given bronze swords, copper-headed spears and wood and leather shields. At first these primitive weapons were no match for the more advanced weaponry of the Hyksos or the Hittites. But the Egyptians learned lessons from this situation, which they later put to good use.

OFFENCE, DEFENCE
Borrowing from the enemy

To increase their effectiveness in battle and gain superiority over their enemies, the Egyptians adopted some of their opponents' weapons and tactics and in effect defeated them with their own methods. In place of the simple curved bow, the Egyptians adopted the composite bow, which the Hyksos had used against them. Later on, they borrowed the double bow from the Hittites together with the tasselled helmet and body armour, which comprised a short-sleeved leather jacket covered in metal plates.

WEAPONS OF ANCIENT EGYPT
The khopesh sword

The bronze swords and other weapons initially used by the Egyptians were an improvement on copper, which was softer, but still they fell somewhat short of requirements in the heat of battle. The Egyptians therefore adopted a heavier curved sword, which was much harder-wearing and could be honed to a sharper edge. This was known as the *khopesh* sword, which, it is believed, developed from the sickle. The *khopesh* was principally a slashing weapon and images from Ancient Egyptian tombs frequently show warriors – always a pharaoh – with sword raised high for this purpose. It has been said that a *khopesh* could not only slice into a helmet with ease, but make the helmet collapse.

THE DEFENCE OF ANCIENT EGYPT
Forts and fortresses

Forts were built in Ancient Egypt from very early times. Not all of them were defensive, but could be built simply to act as a warning of the strength and power a pharaoh could bring against would-be rebels. This was probably the purpose of the first Ancient Egyptian fort constructed during the Old Kingdom (2686–2181 BC) at Buhen in Nubia. But for obvious reasons, the greater number of defensive forts were constructed when the Egyptians were extending their power during the Middle Kingdom (2055–1659 BC). A chain of forts, protected wells and waterholes and were strung out along Egypt's borders only a day's march apart to prevent sneak incursions by potential enemies.

ANCIENT EGYPTIAN WARFARE
Strategy and tactics

Generally speaking, the Ancient Egyptian army did not favour pitched-battle tactics when confronting an enemy. Instead, confrontations were more subtle. At the battle of Qadesh (1294 BC), for instance, there was a preliminary skirmish after which the Egyptian and Hittite contestants decided that neither of them could win: instead, they negotiated a truce. Sieges were more brutal, but even so, backdoor tactics were frequently preferred. The Egyptians opted for attrition, starvation or battering rams to wear down their enemies and hammer their way in rather than fight it out on the battlements.

LIFE IN THE EGYPTIAN ARMY
A long tour of service

There was only one way for the Egyptian army to be deployed – the slow, hard way. Within Egyptian territory, troops and their provisions were moved by ship. Reaching outside destinations, however, required a long series of gruelling marches. The troops could cover a basic 22 km (14 m) per day but this was often slowed down by the need for the men to take provisions from the countryside through which they passed. Camping at night required the building of a wall made of shields before the troops could settle down to sleep in reasonable safety. They shared the protected space with their pack animals.

The Pharaoh's Chariots

FAST TRANSPORT WARFARE
The pharaoh's chariots

The chariot was by far the most important weapon that the Ancient Egyptians copied from their enemies. It took warfare into a new, faster era and through the speed of its assaults also introduced a new terror to warfare. The Egyptians first saw the chariot and the havoc it could wreak during their struggle against the Hyksos (*c.* 1800–1600 BC). Before long, they were building up their own corps of chariots, acquiring them either through trade or capturing them in battle. This, of course, gave the Egyptians plenty of models on which to base the design of their own chariots.

CHARIOTS AS BOOTY

Captured at Megiddo

The capture of enemy chariots by the Egyptian army reached vast proportions at the battle of Megiddo (1469 BC). In fact, the total was almost three times as many chariots as the prisoners they captured. Two chariots of exceptional quality were among the booty – both wrought in gold, one of them with a golden pole. These chariots comprised a crucial loss to the enemies of the Pharaoh Thutmose III (1479–1425 BC) – the rebellious chieftains of Palestine, who were overwhelmingly defeated.

ADAPTING THE CHARIOT
The Egyptian chariot

Syrian chariots were heavy and difficult to control. To improve their performance, the Egyptians made them lighter and also stronger by constructing them from woods like birch and ash. They also replaced the cumbersome wheels of the Syrian chariot by giving them lighter spokes radiating from a central hub. The Egyptian chariot had a wicker platform, which gave its passengers a very bumpy ride as it sped over rough terrain. Subsequently the wicker platform was replaced by a primitive 'shock absorber' made of leather.

RIDING THE CHARIOT
Driver and archer

The chariots, which were open at the back to allow for quick entry and exit, carried up to two men: the driver in front and an archer behind him. Basically, a war chariot was an unstable vehicle so that the driver needed to be highly skilled and know how to handle his horses. The archer required a good sense of balance since his hands would be fully occupied wielding his bow. Two quivers full of arrows and twelve short spears were strapped to the chariot for his use.

THE HERALDRY OF THE CHARIOT

Distinguishing friend from foe

Charioteers and archers could face danger from what is now termed 'friendly fire' – the failure of their own side to recognize them. It was all too easy in the clash and crush of battle to mistake friend for foe, and a simple form of heraldry was introduced to ensure this did not happen. The horses were caparisoned in brightly coloured coats which carried the coat of arms of their owner. Other distinguishing features comprised ostrich feathers, artificial flowers or coloured streamers.

THE CHARIOT BRIGADES

One fifth of the army

During the New Kingdom, which began with the 18th Dynasty in around 1550 BC, the chariot force accounted for roughly a fifth of the manpower in each of the three divisions making up the army. There were about 1,000 chariots to 4,000 infantry. A chariot contingent was led by a marshal and was divided into brigades. Each brigade comprised two squadrons; five companies of ten chariots each constituted a squadron. The archers assigned to the chariots came from the army divisions, which were named after gods: the Seth division (the heroic archers) or the Amun division (the mighty archers). A third division was named after the sun god Ra (the many-armed).

The Legacy of Ancient Egypt

KNOWLEDGE AND SCIENCE
Egyptian trailblazers

The legacy of the Ancient Egyptian civilization is all-pervading. It helped lead the way in a vast number of directions – to art, science and scientific methods, architecture, mathematics and astronomy. The Egyptians developed working in bronze, precision surveying, plumbing with copper, algebraic equations and, as early as around 3100 BC, the use of the decimal numbering system. These, though, were only a few of the achievements of Ancient Egypt. There were many more.

DECORATION
Glass work

Glass was frequently used in Ancient Egypt for inlays, amulets and beads, but more often appeared as decorations on larger objects. Although glass blowing was not known in Egypt until Roman times, after around 30 BC, glassworkers made some beautiful pieces by other methods, such as core forming. A core of sand and mud was dipped into molten glass, then the surface evened out by rolling it on a flat stone. Colour was applied in the form of delicate blue or blue-green threads. Decorations in yellow, red, white, orange and other colours were added by trailing a needle over the still-soft glass.

FAÏENCE
The world's first earthenware

Faïence, which had a delicate quality highlighted by its soda coating, or turquoise or green glaze, was made from crushed quartz or quartz sand together with small quantities of plant ash, lime or natron. It was already being used in pre-dynastic times up to 7,000 years ago to make small figurines, amulets, inlays, vessels and ornaments on buildings. *Shabtis* – the models of servants found in Ancient Egyptian tombs – were frequently made of faïence.

ANIMAL HUSBANDRY
Beekeeping

The Ancient Egyptians regarded bees as the tears of the sun god Ra. Bees had a considerable significance in Egyptian culture: their honey was used as an important sweetener for food and also in medicine where it served as an anti-bacterial base for unguents. Beeswax was useful, too, in moulding wax images for casting metal. Beekeeping could be big business in Ancient Egypt, with a healthy export trade and a network of apiaries serving local communities. Honey was also taken from the wild bees that swarmed around the desert fringes, though this could be dangerous work suitable only for professional beekeepers. Bees, beekeeping and hives were illustrated on pottery and also in private tombs.

COMMUNICATION
Egyptian Hieroglyphs

'Hieroglyphs', which means 'sacred carved letters' in Greek, were used in Ancient Egypt from around 3200 BC. Some of these 'signs' were used as pictures (or 'ideograms'), but most writing was done with signs representing consonants (either one, two or three), supplemented by a sign representing the word group. Many signs had both a phonetic and a picture value. Birds, for example, were best recognized in profile so their hieroglyphs presented them that way. More abstract words used sign language to impart their meanings: the verb 'to answer', for instance, indicated a man holding his hand in his mouth. Hieroglyphs were written from right to left in continuous lines but without punctuation or any other indication of where a sentence began or ended.

TIME
The Egyptian calendar

The Ancient Egyptian astronomical calendar, which had a 360-day year and twelve months of 30 days each, has been traced back to at least 2700 BC, but was probably in use before that. But it was only after around 2055 BC that the months, which had three 'weeks' lasting ten days each, were given names instead of numbers. The calendar had the extra five days added to the end of the year and was split into the three seasons that began with *akhet*, the inundation of the Nile, followed by *peret*, the growing period and *shemu*, harvest time. The Egyptian calendar was considered so accurate that it was still being used by astronomers some 4,000 years later, in medieval Europe.

INDEX

Page numbers in *italics* indicate pictures.